Bolivia

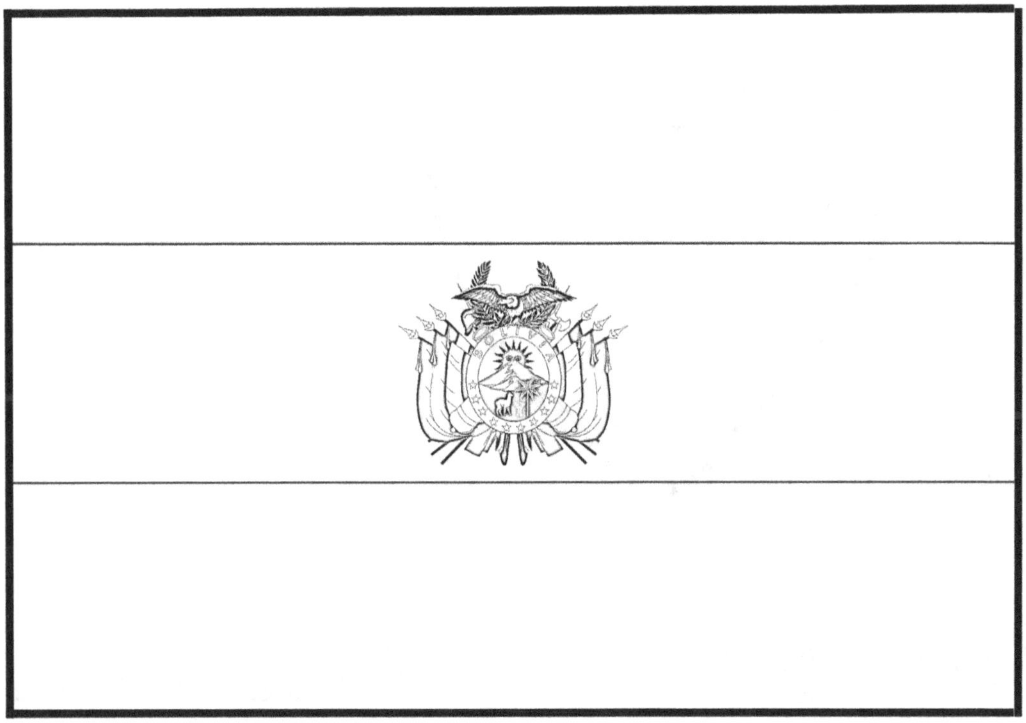

The national flag colors are red(top), yellow(middle) and green(bottom) with the coat of arms in the middle.

Bolivia is a great country located at the heart of South America.

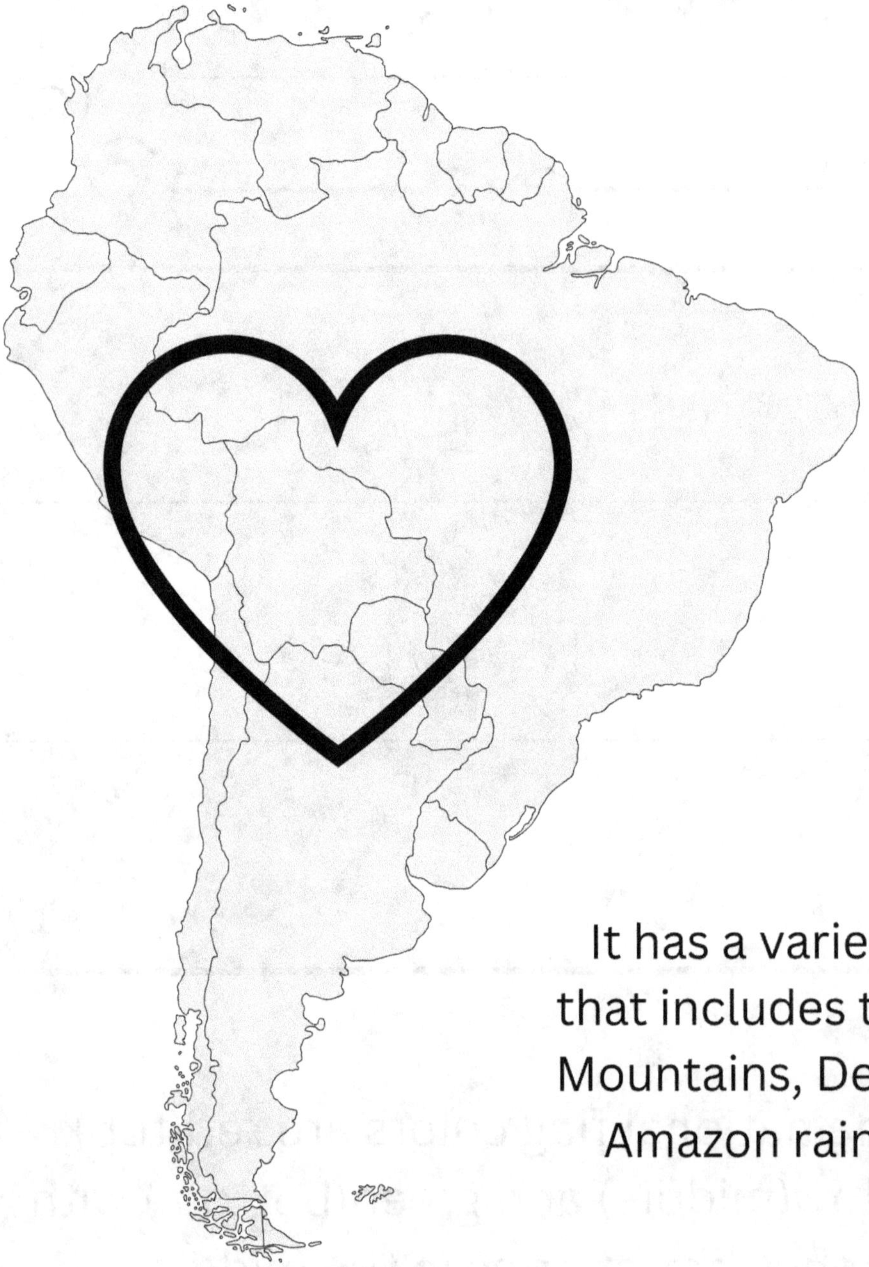

It has a varied terrain that includes the Andes Mountains, Deserts and Amazon rainforest.

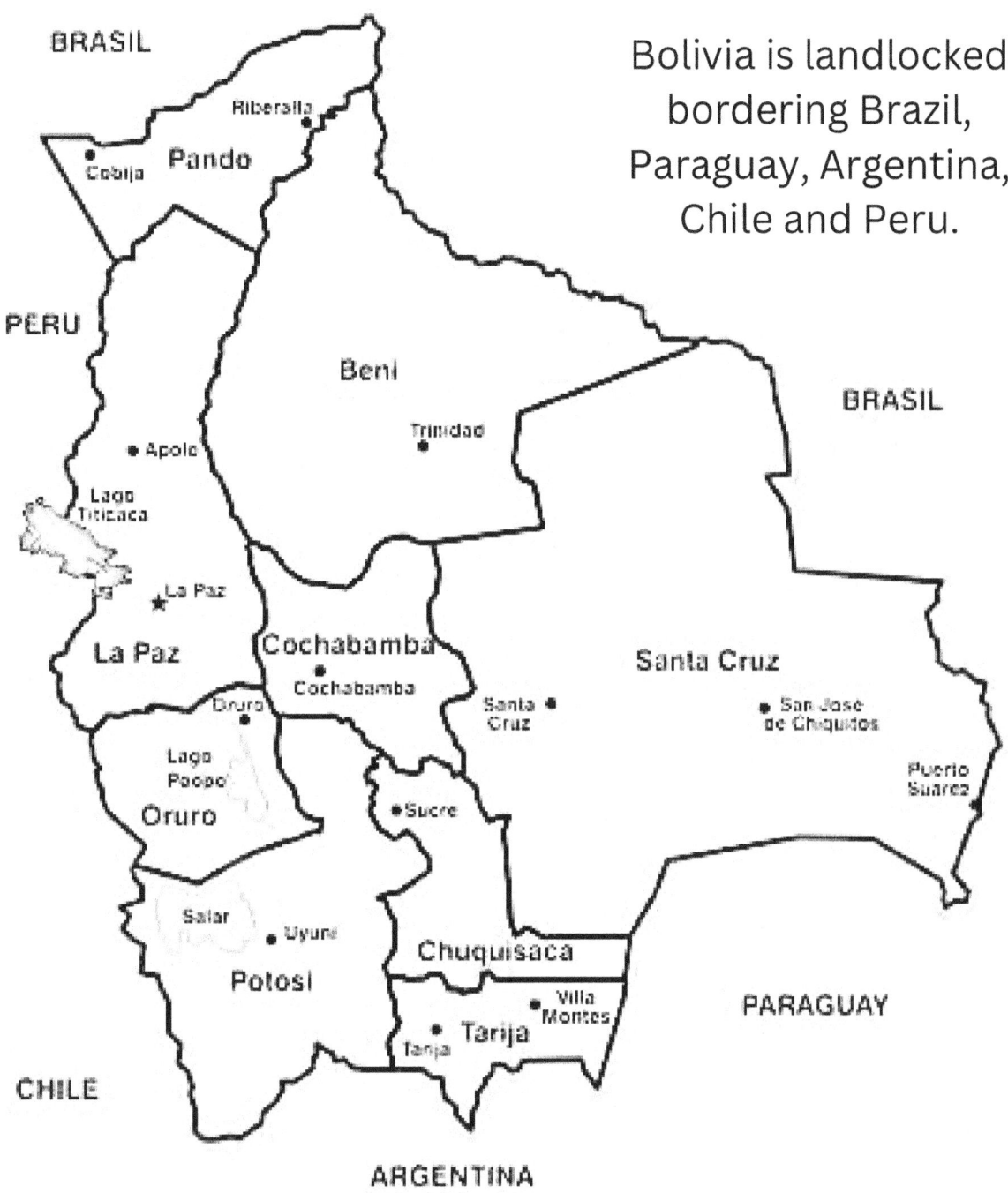

Bolivia is landlocked bordering Brazil, Paraguay, Argentina, Chile and Peru.

Bolivia has nine departments :
Pando, Beni, Santa Cruz, Cochabamba, La Paz, Chuquisaca., Oruro, Potosi, and Tarija

The Kantua also called "flower of the Incas" is the national flower, it is found in high valleys.

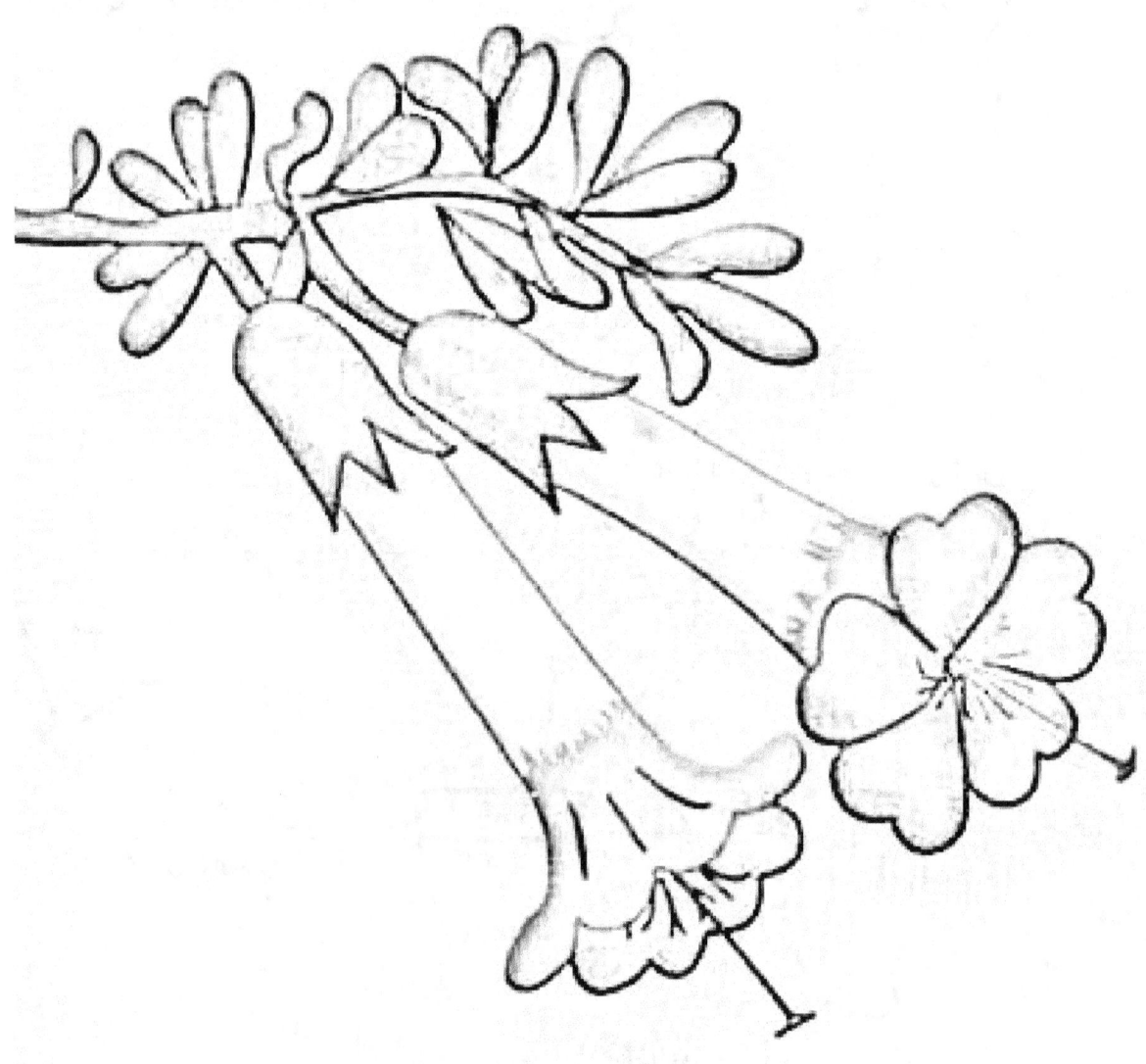

The colors of the Kantua are the same as the national flag: the red flower, the yellow middle part and the green leaves.

Pando

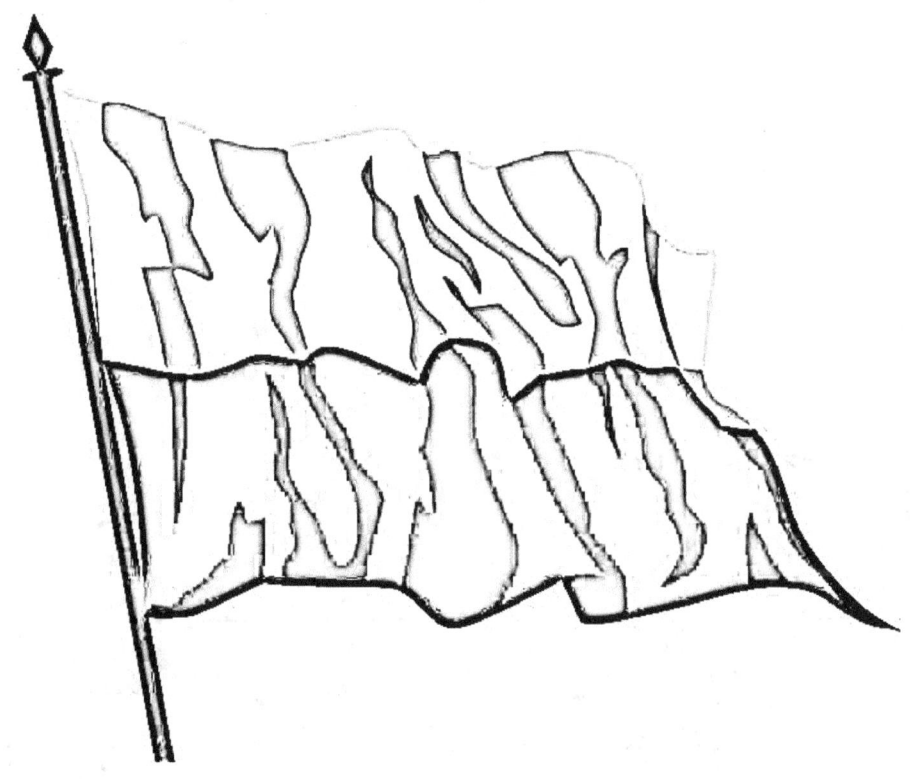

Pando's flag is made up of two horizontal stripes of equal dimensions: the upper stripe is white and the lower stripe is green with the coat of arms

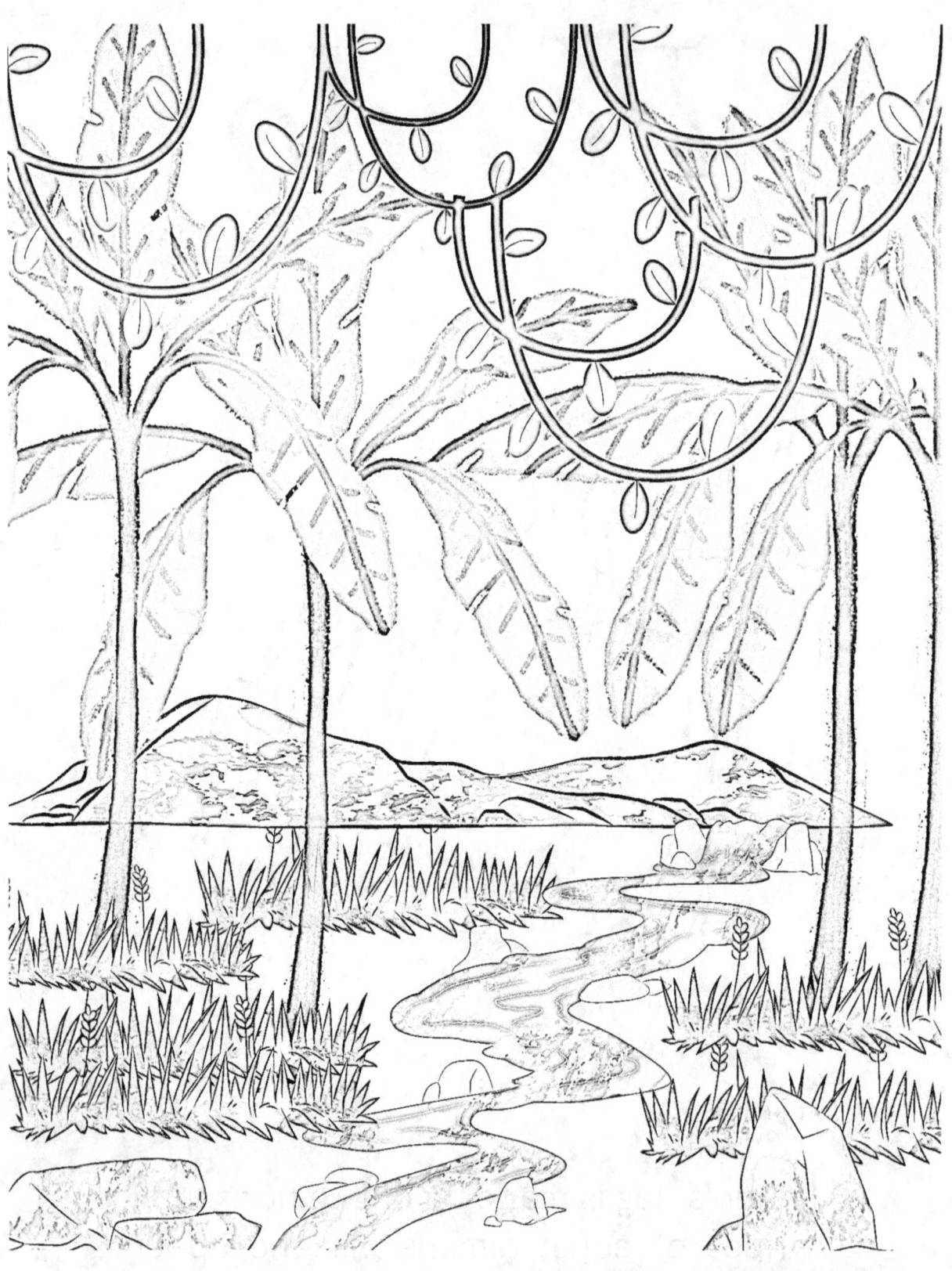

Pando has a tropical climate and is covered by the Amazon jungle and crossed by innumerable rivers.

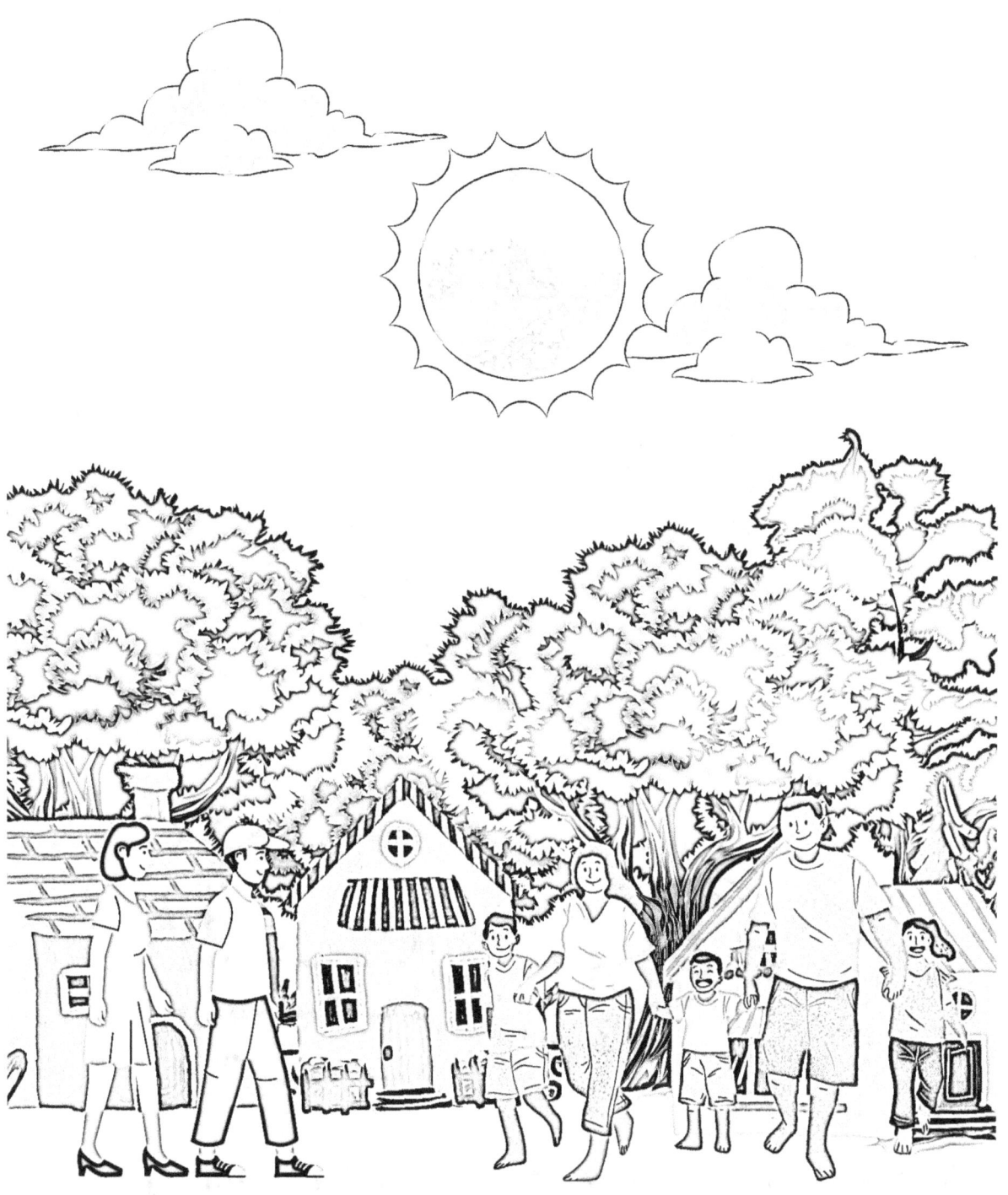

The department of Pando has an average temperature of 80 °F which is very pleasant for walks in the surrounding area.

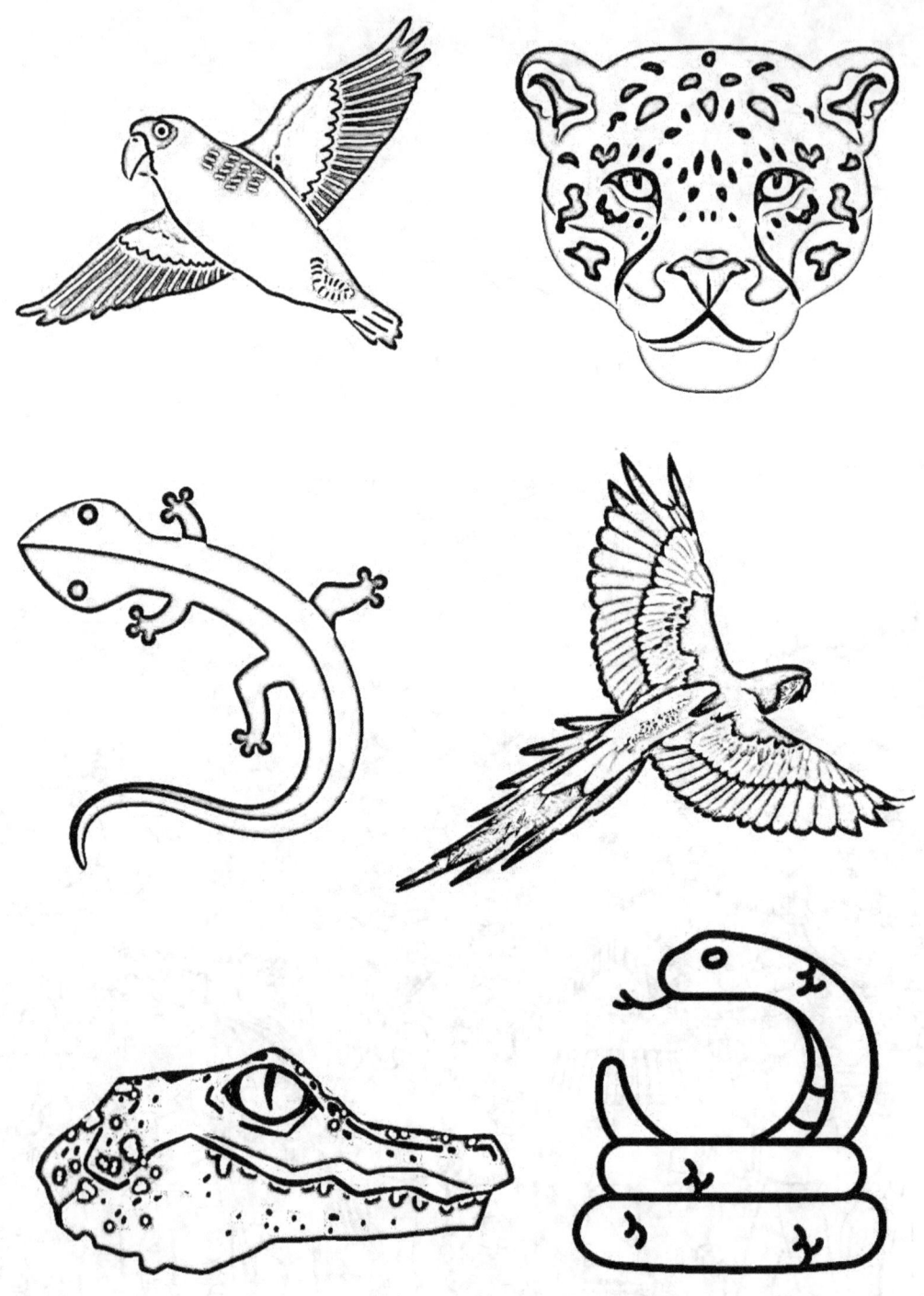

Animal in the area: wild cat, badger, puma, jaguar, monkeys, anteaters, caiman lizards, iguanas, anacondas, a variety of viper species, poisonous snakes and an extensive variety of birds.

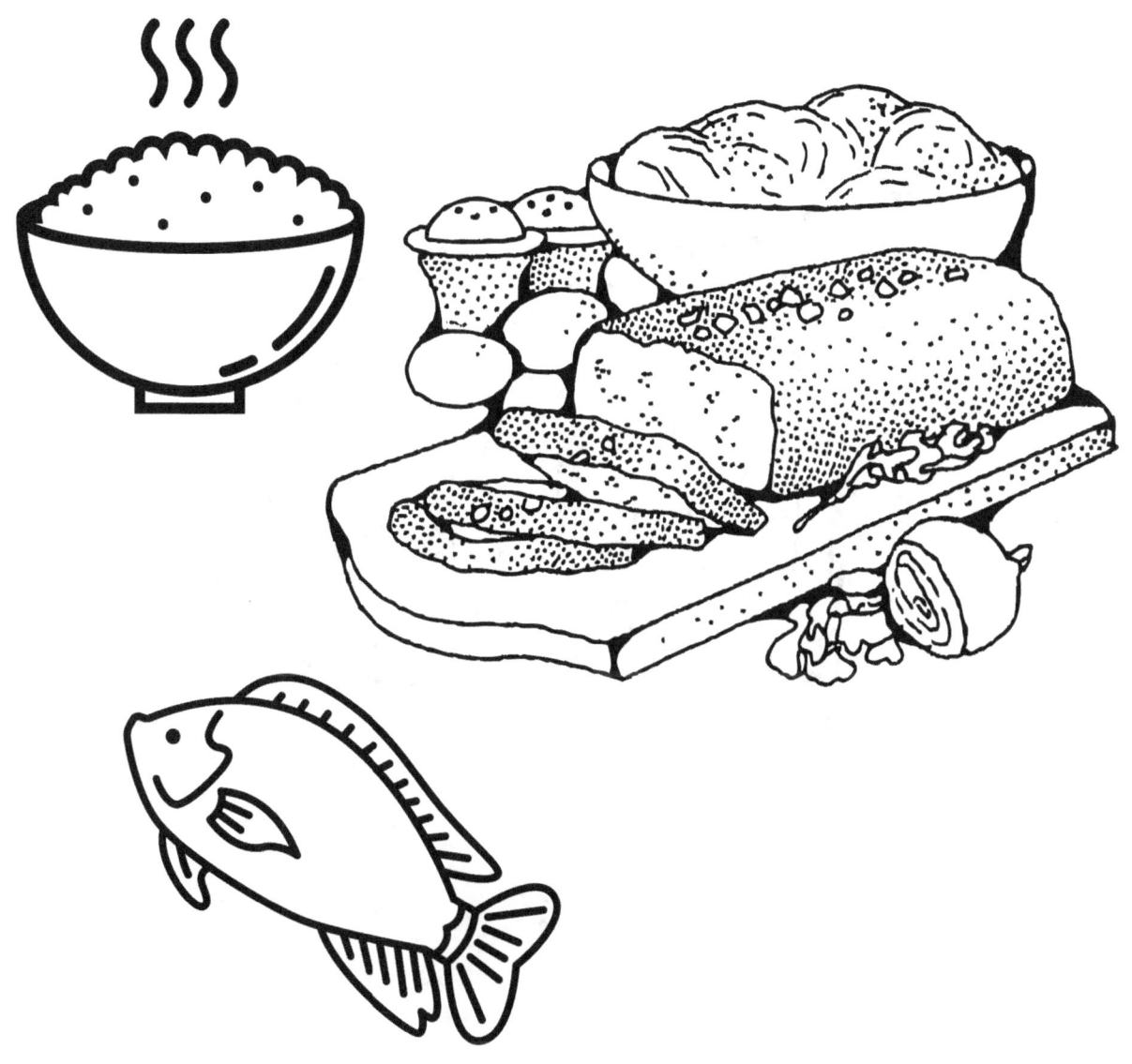

Typical dishes from the department of Pando are Farofa, marinade of Torcaza, Meat of Moroco, Sudado de Surubí, Keperí, Rice Pie.

La Paz

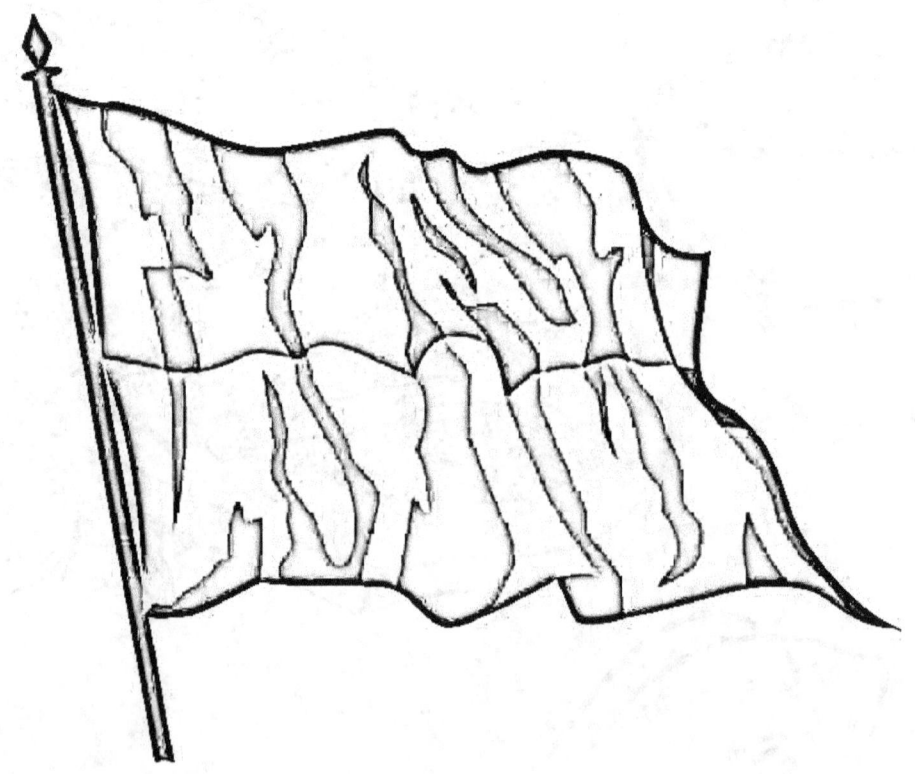

La Paz's flag is made up of two horizontal stripes of equal dimensions: the upper stripe is red and the lower stripe is dark green with the coat of arms in the middle.

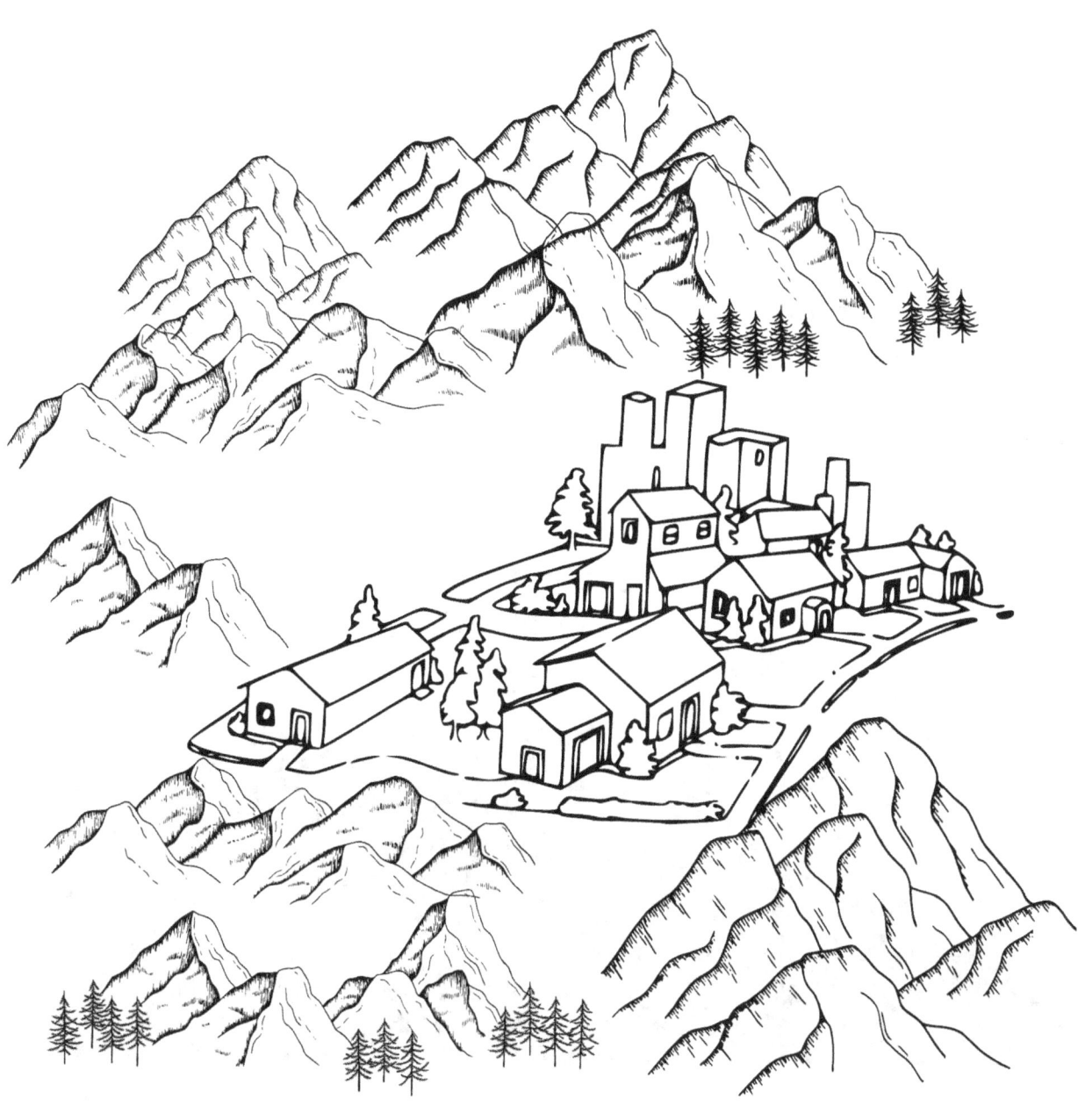

Located in western Bolivia, it is situated in a canyon created by the Choqueyapu River and is surrounded by the high mountains of the altiplano.

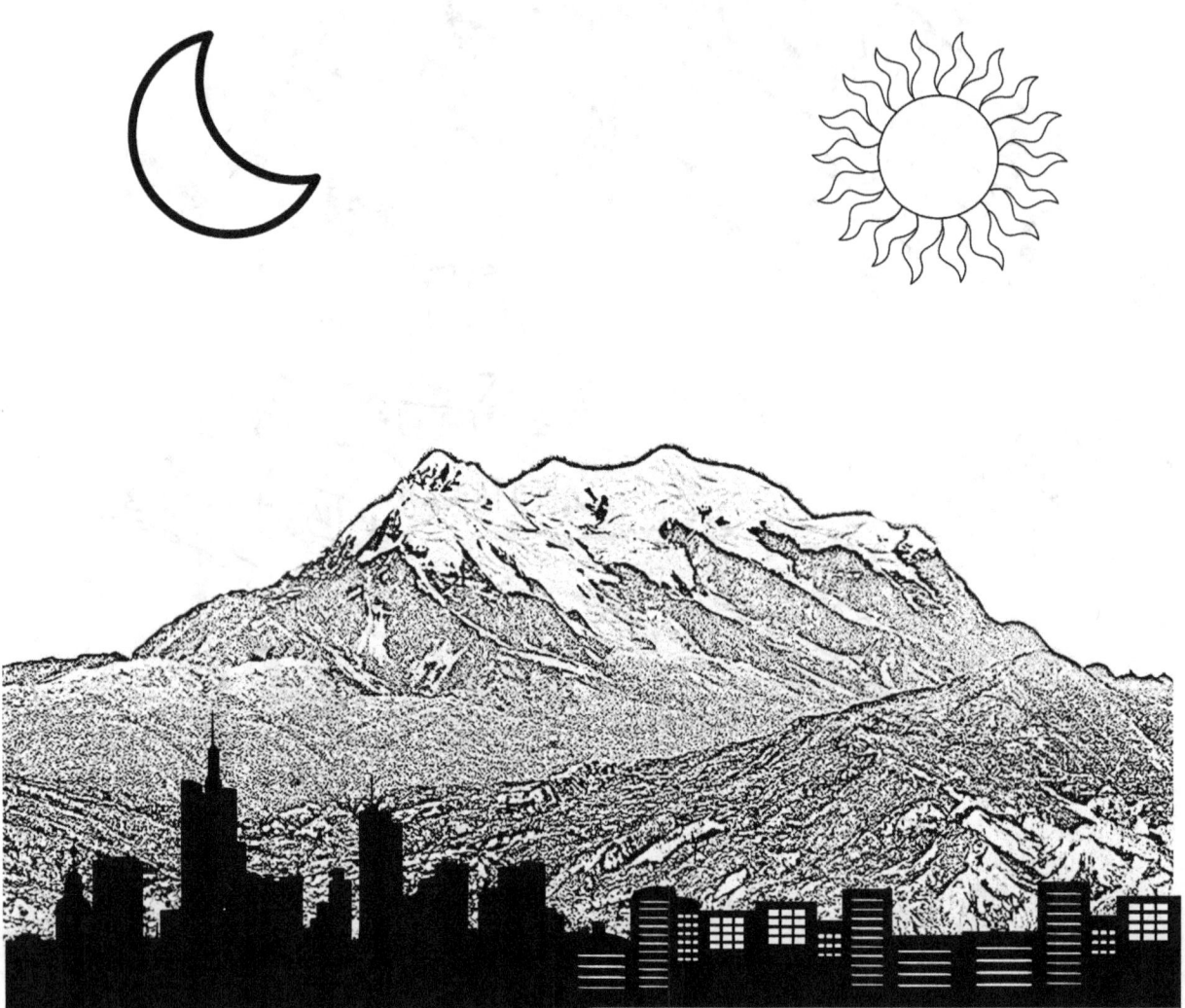

Among these mountains, is the highest mountain in the Cordillera Real, the snowy Illimani, whose silhouette has been an important emblem of the city since its foundation.

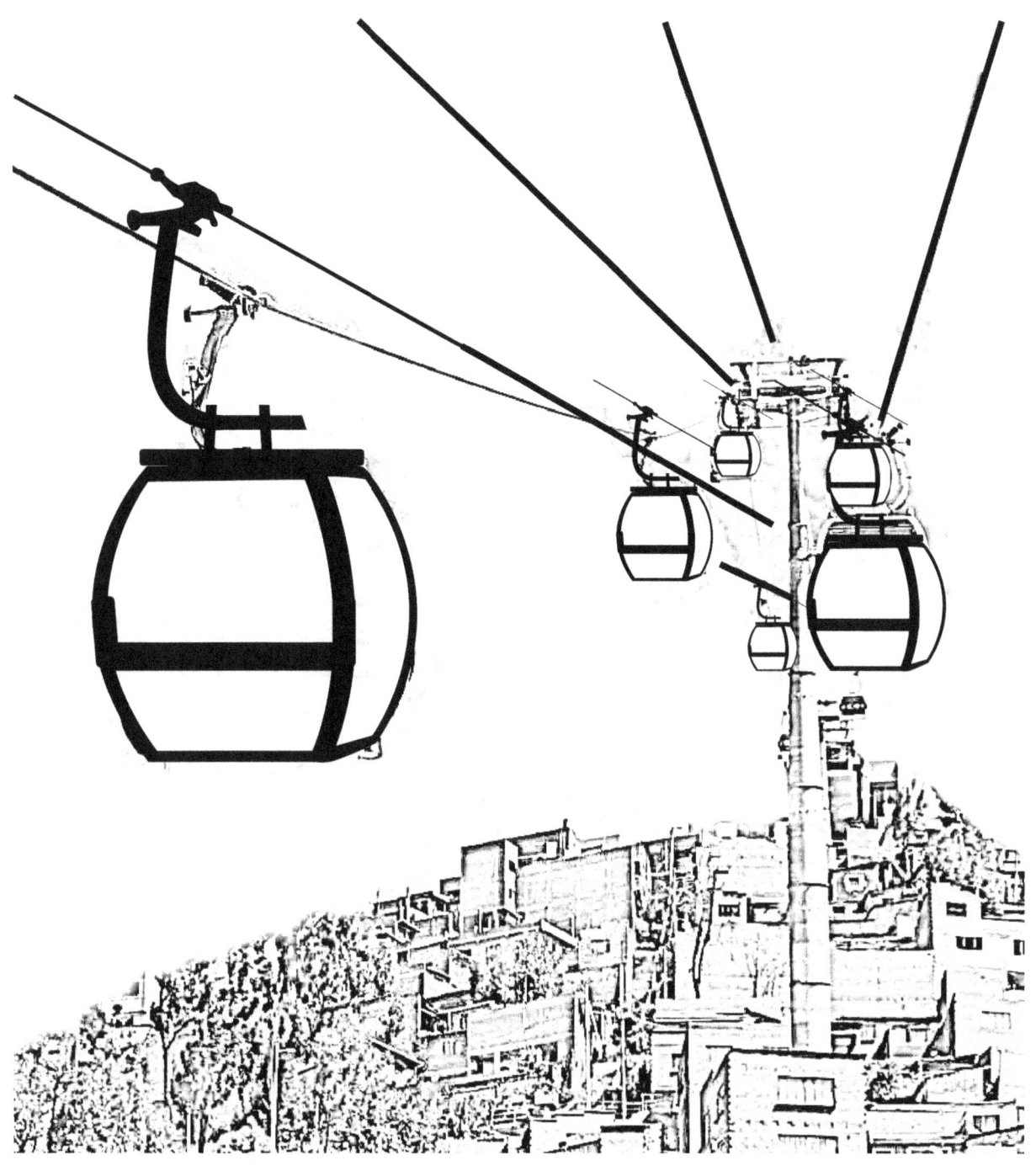

The Teleférico (cable car) in La Paz, is a cable system that connects the whole city by air, avoiding the traffic jams of this city.

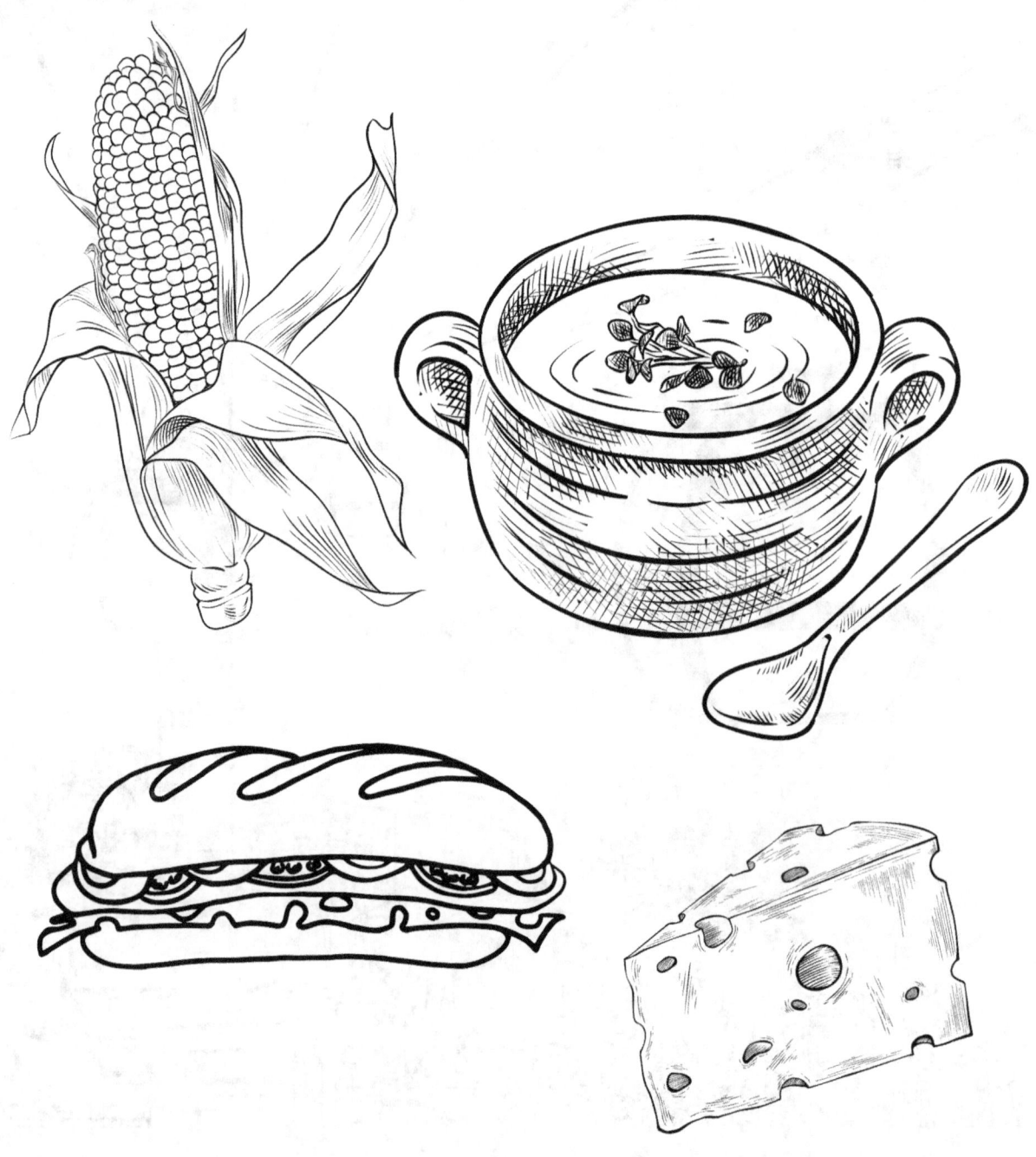

Typical dishes from the department are: Plato paceño, Chairo, Fricasé, Queso humacha, Sándwich de chola, Fritanga, Chairo.

Oruro

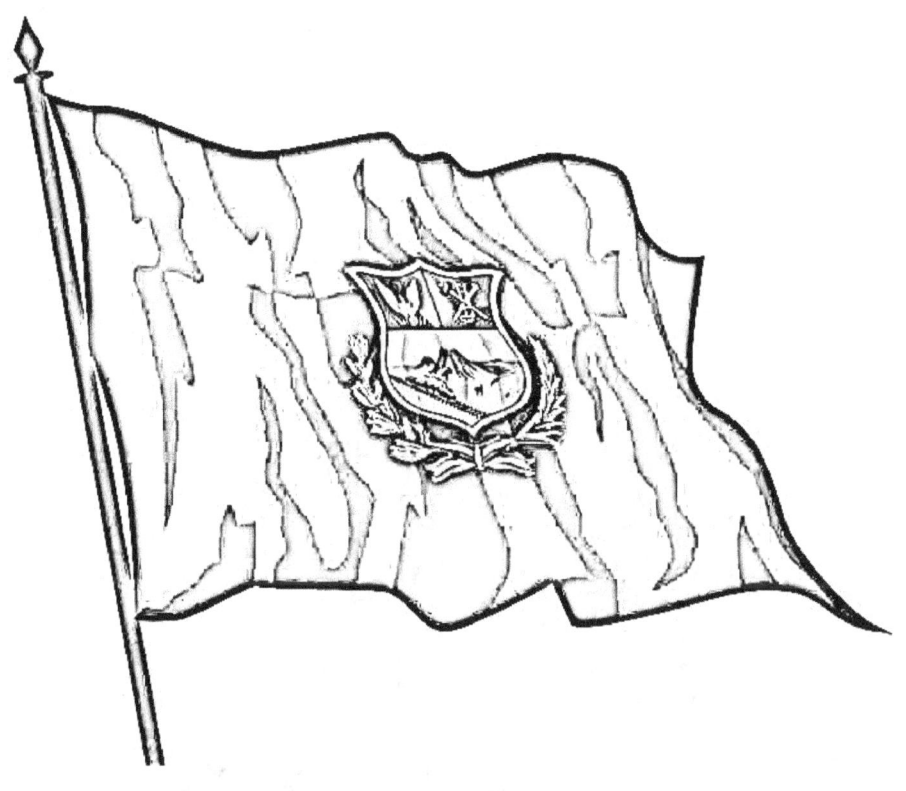

Oruro's flag is Crimson Red with the department's coat of arms in the middle.

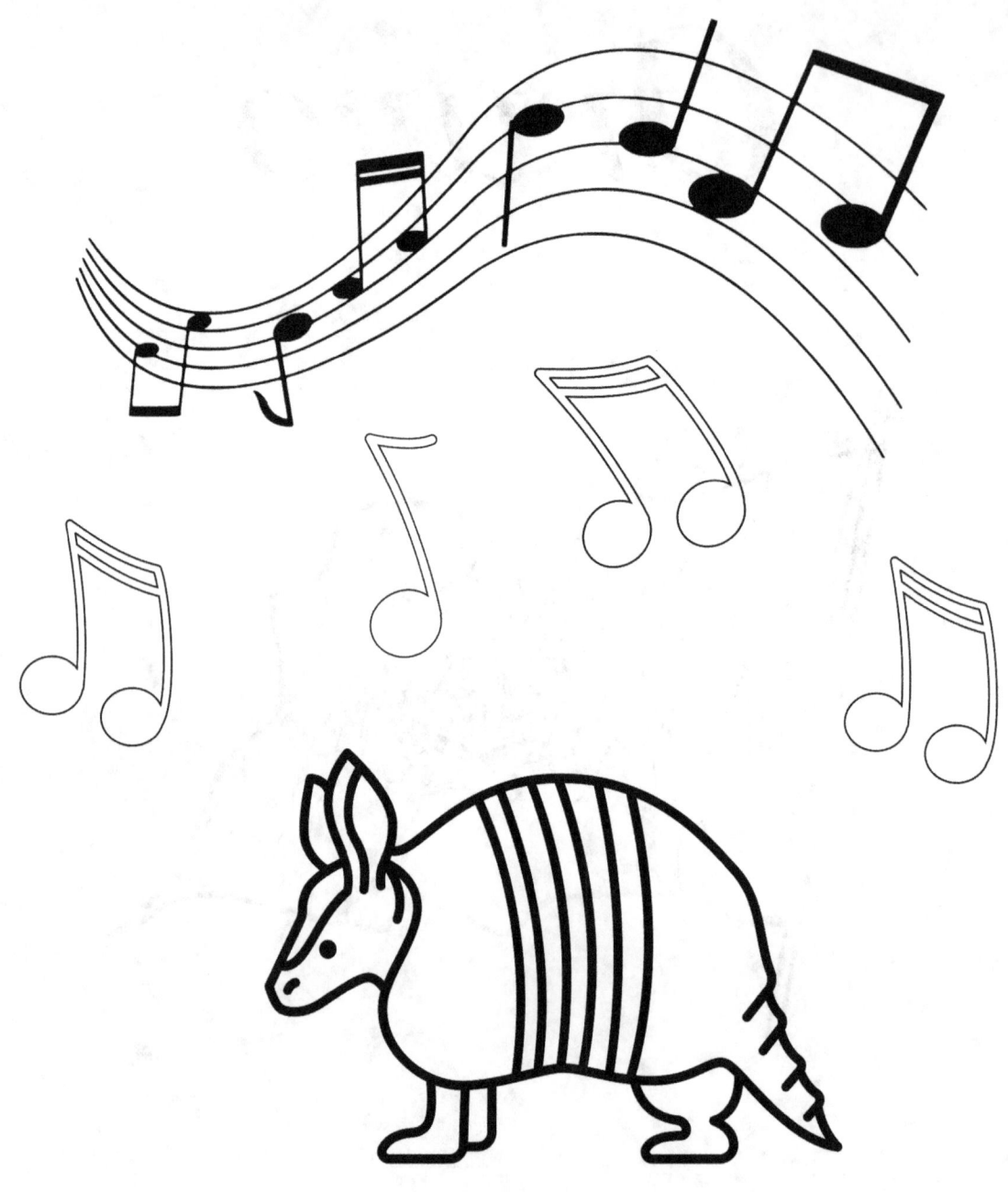

Located in the altiplano, this department has as its emblem the quirquincho (Andean armadillo), whose shell is used to make the charango (Bolivian string instrument, similar to a guitar).

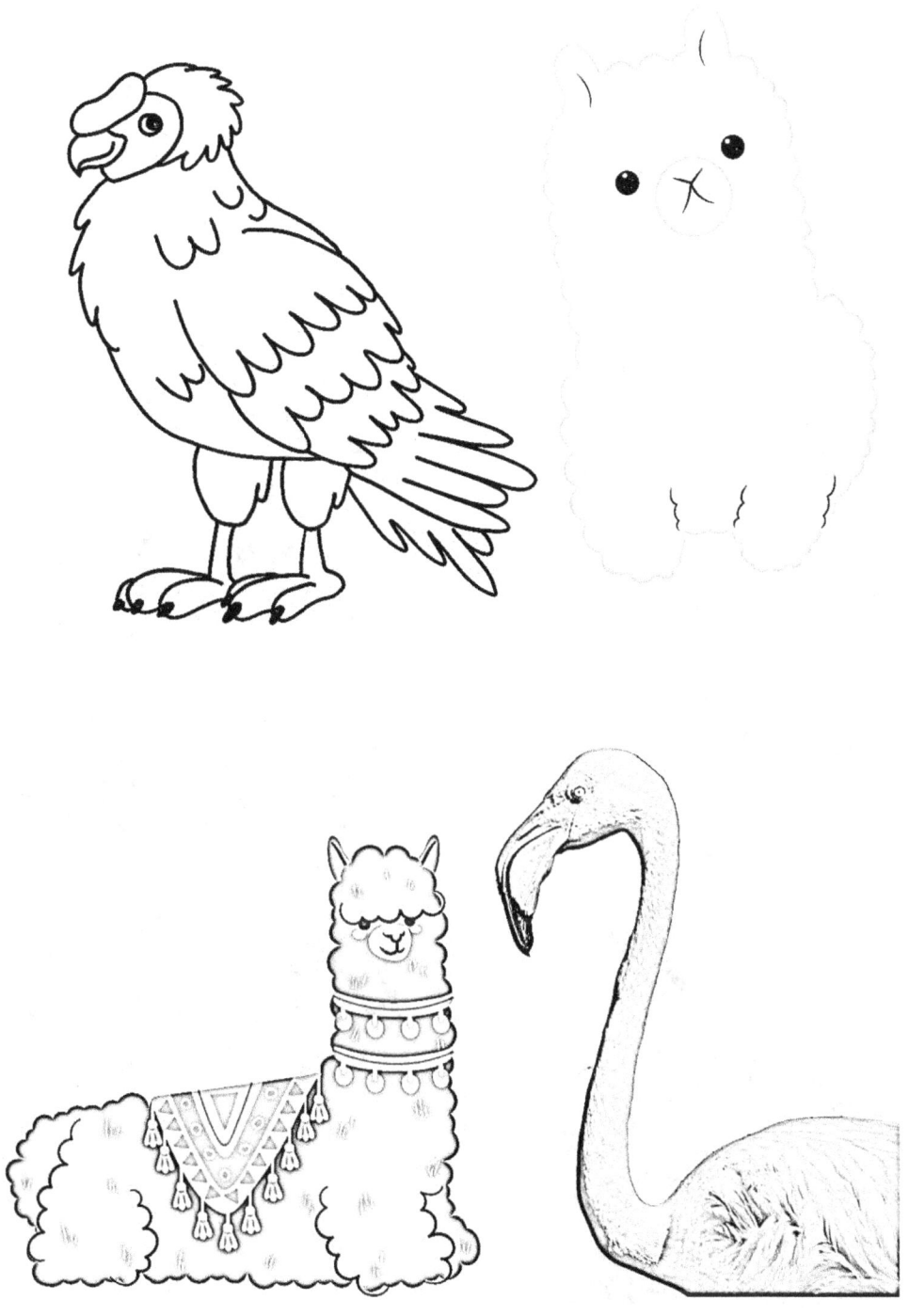

In addition to the quirquincho, its territory is home to a typical fauna of the altiplano: llamas, alpacas, vicuñas, pumas, vizcachas, pink flamingos, condors, etc.

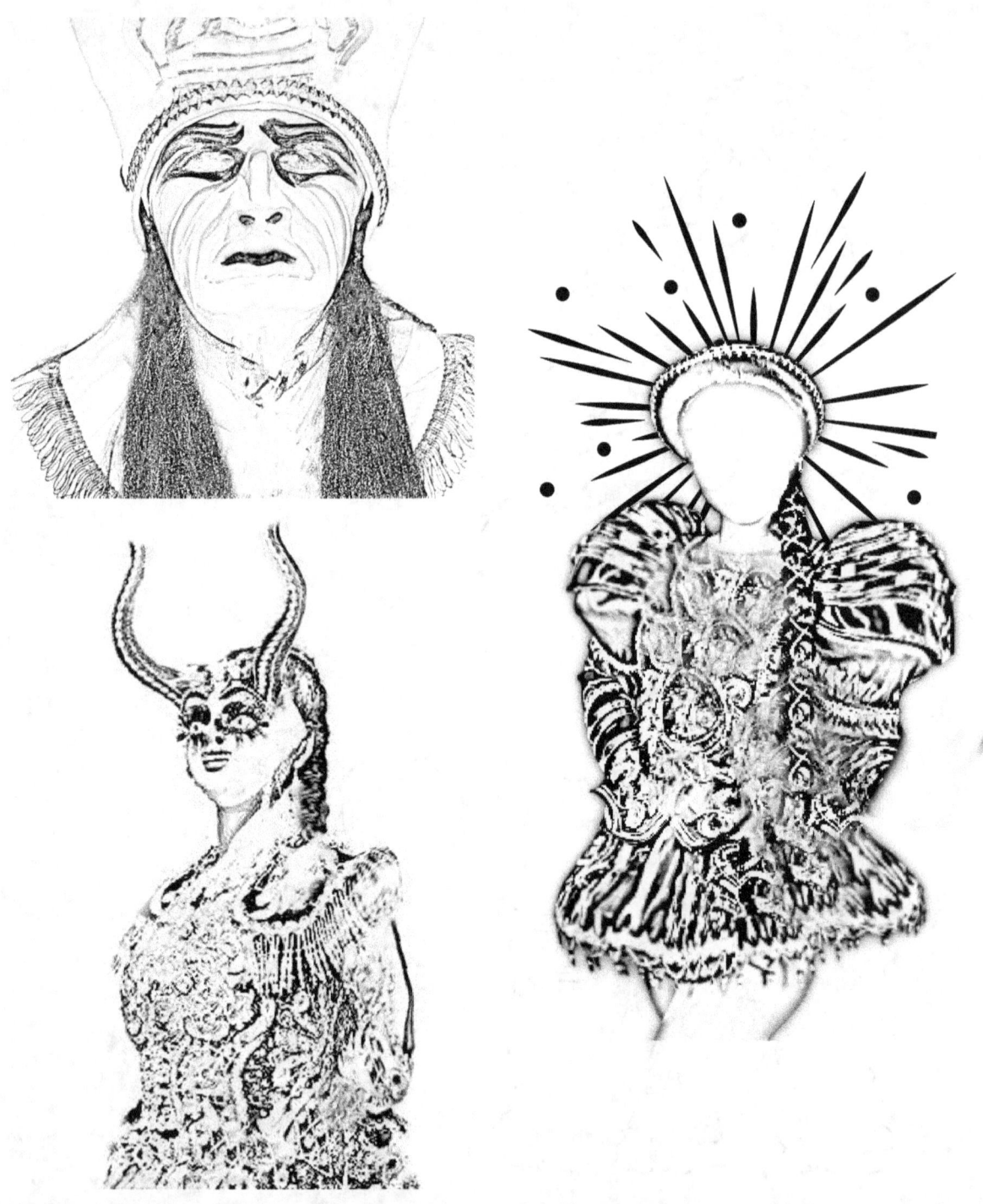

The Oruro carnival is a symbol of Bolivian culture. This famous event welcomes more than a million people every year. It is one of the most unique and oldest carnivals in the world since it has existed for more than 200 years.

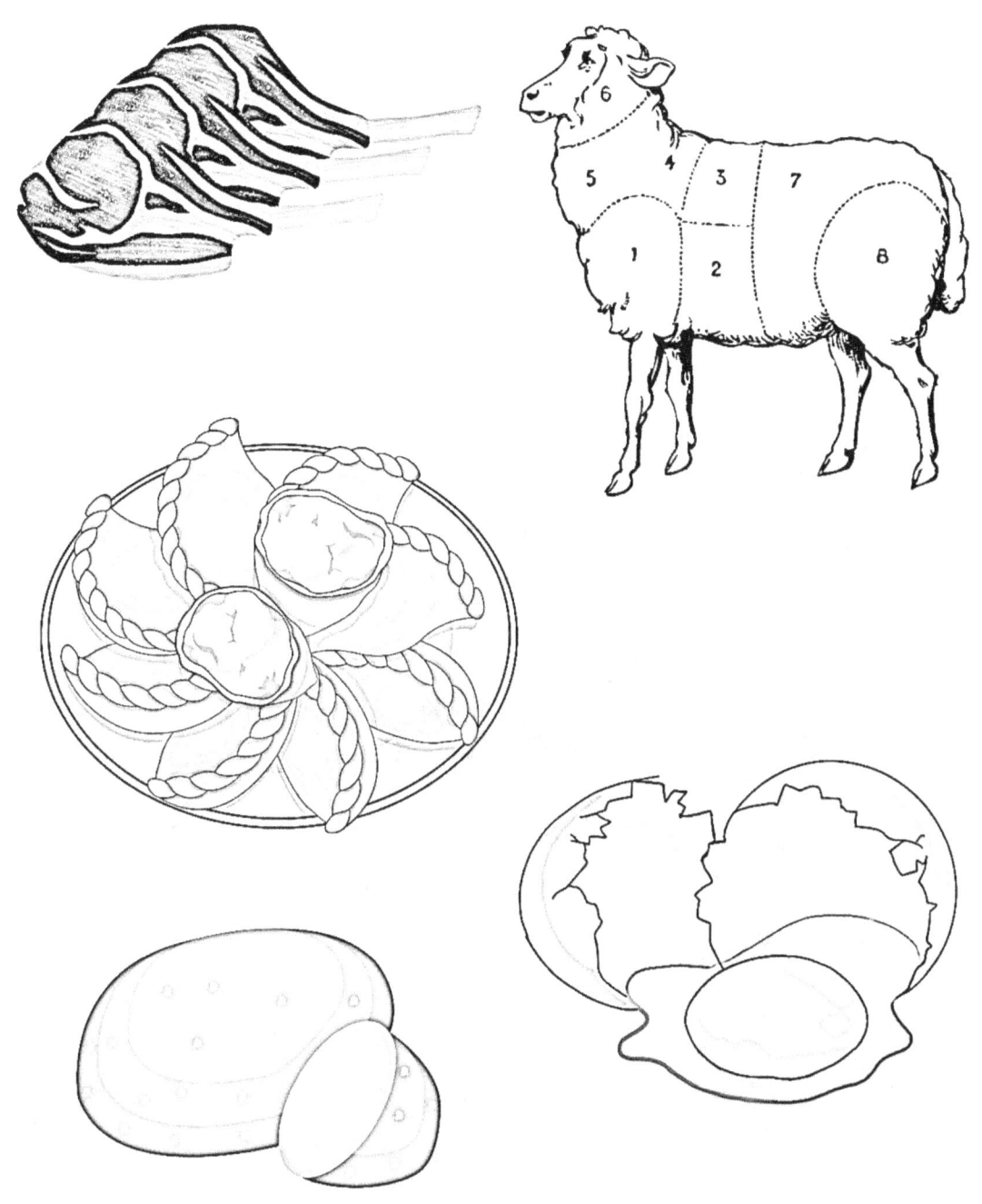

Typical dishes from Oruro : Roasted face, El Intendente, Condori, Charquekan with potatoe , Brazuelo of lamb, Api with fried empanada.

Beni

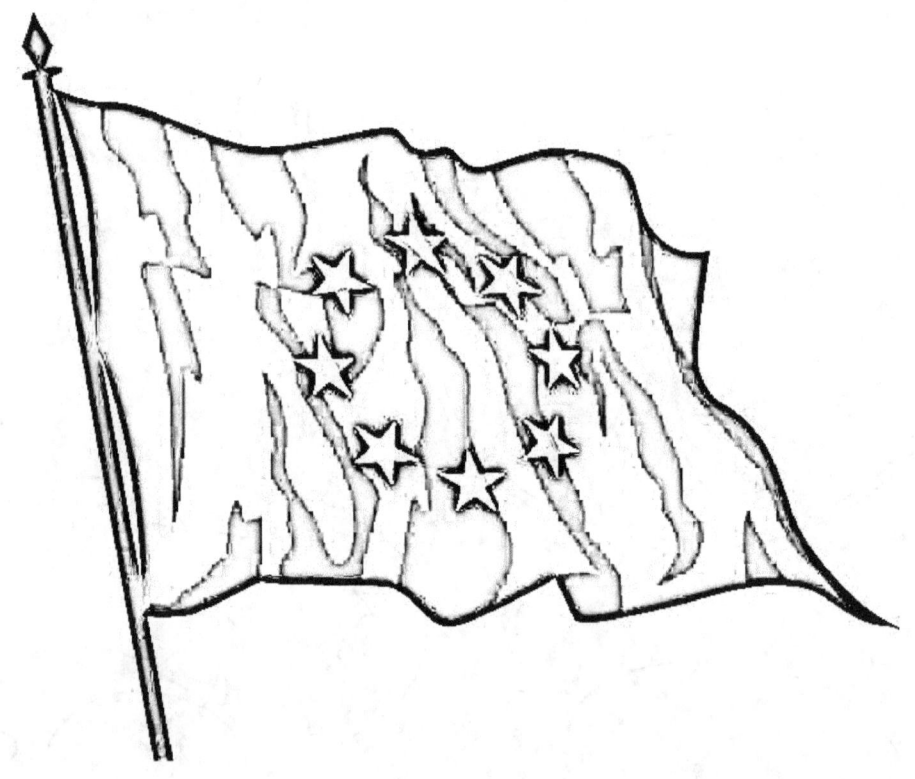

Beni's flag is green with 8 yellows stars that represent the eight provinces of that department.

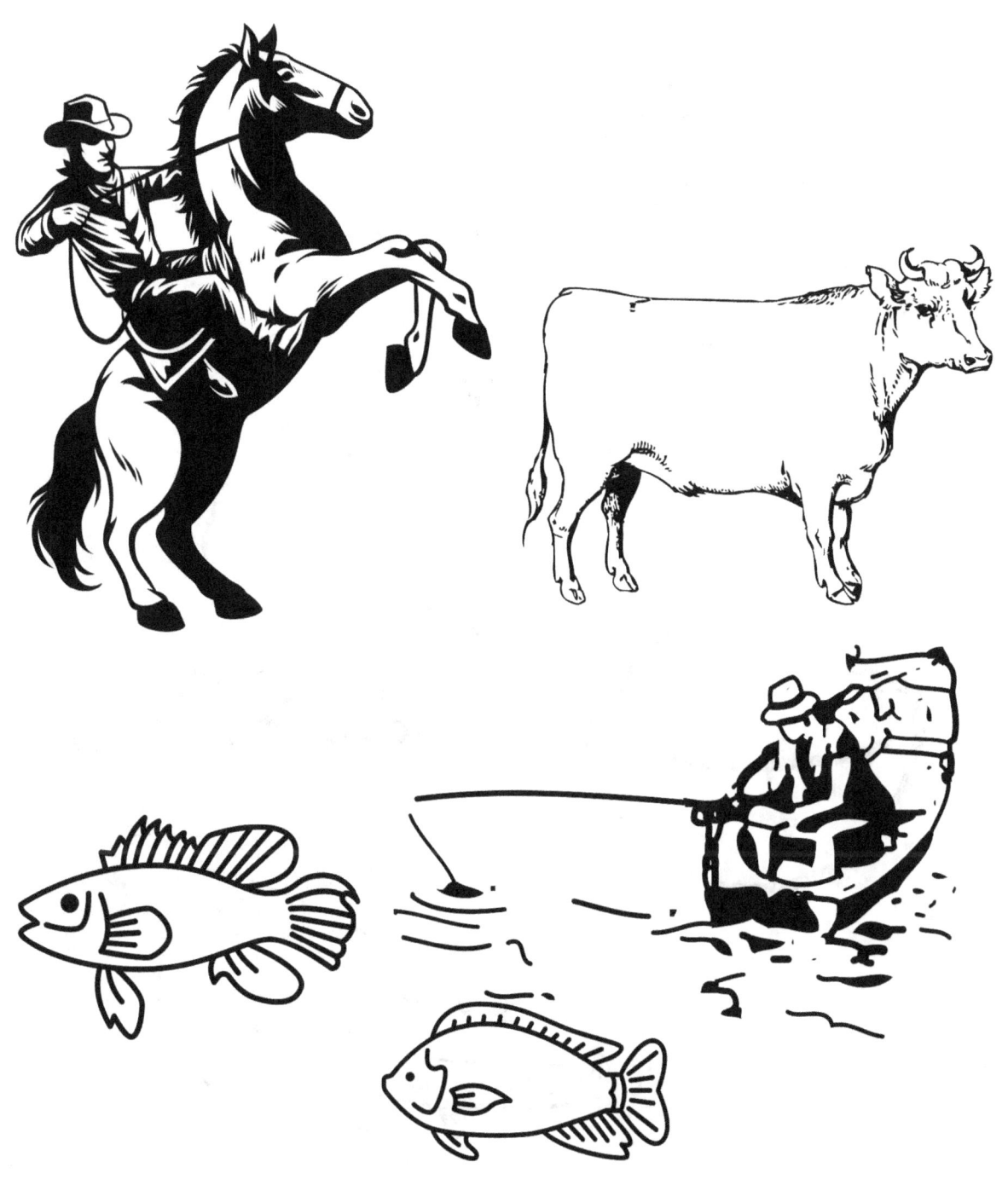

The current population is ethnically diverse. The main economic activities are agriculture, timber, cattle, logging, small-scale fishing, hunting, farming, and in recent years, eco-tourism.

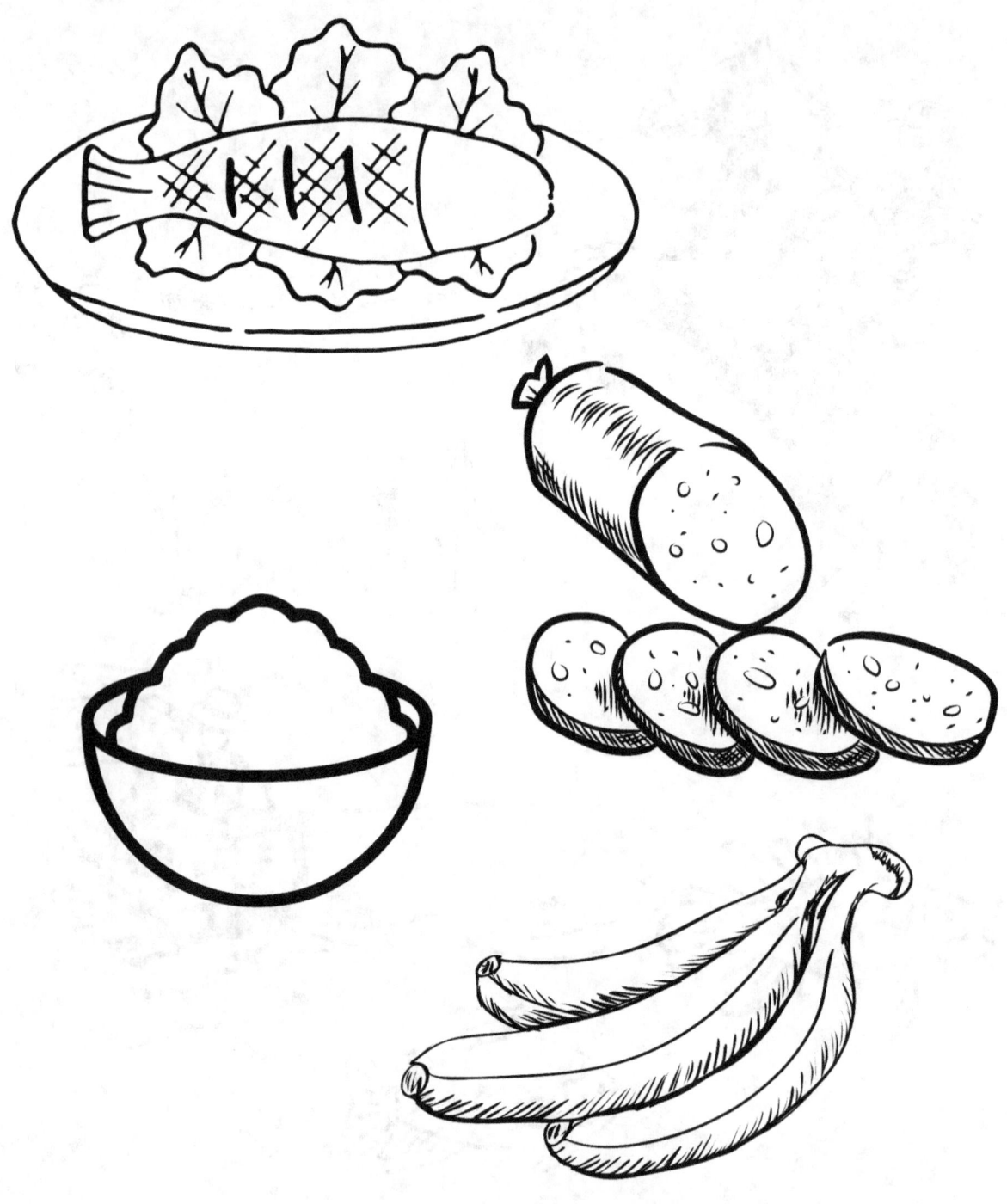

The Beniano's (people from Beni) diet consists largely of rice, bananas, beef, and fish. Typical dishes includes piranha soup , beniano sausage ,Bagre broth, Baked Surubí, Keperi beniano, Masako.

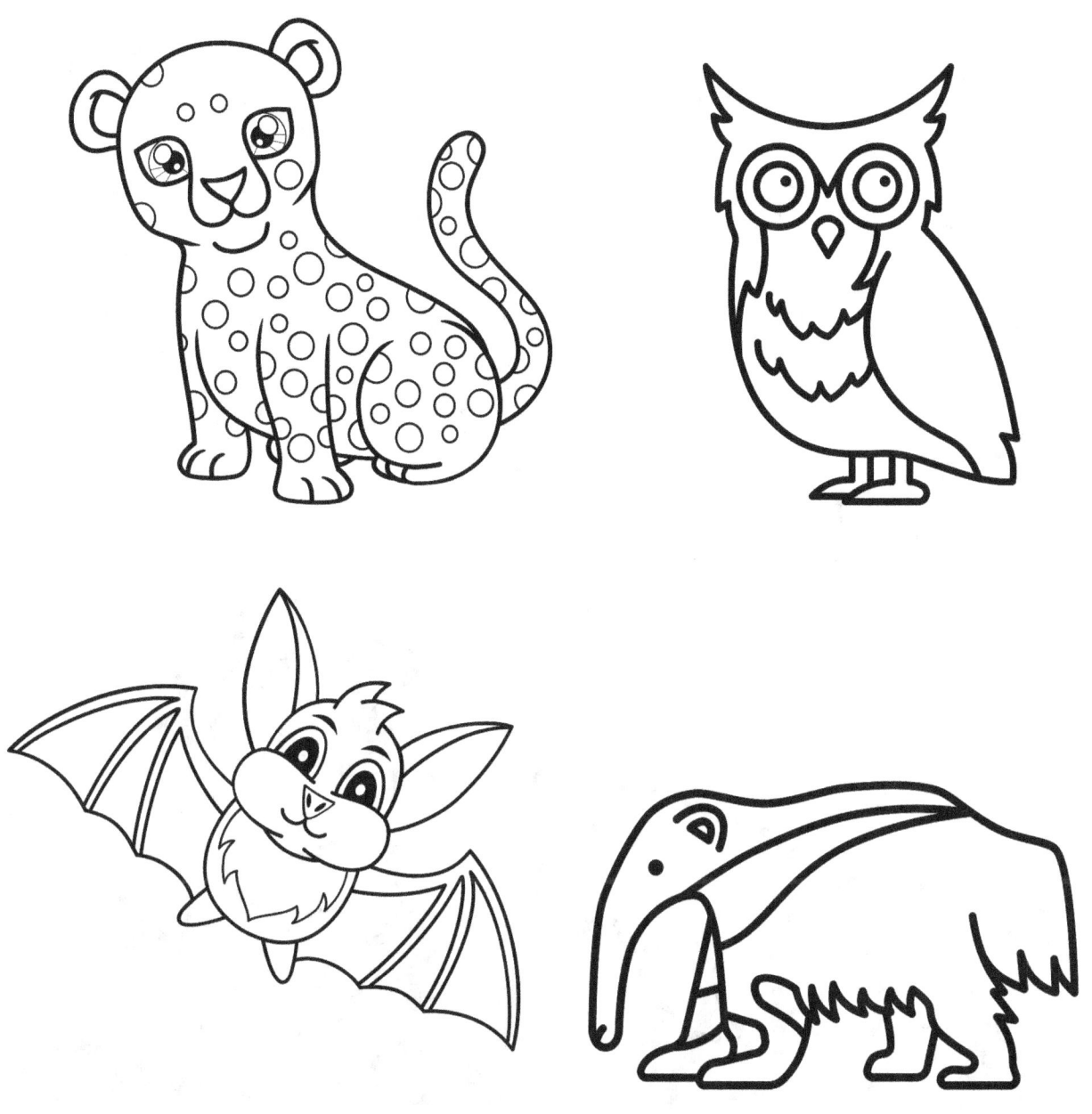

Animals of the region: jaguars, pumas, anteaters, opossums, wild cats, brown bears, taitetú, Jukumari bears, woodpeckers, bats, owls.

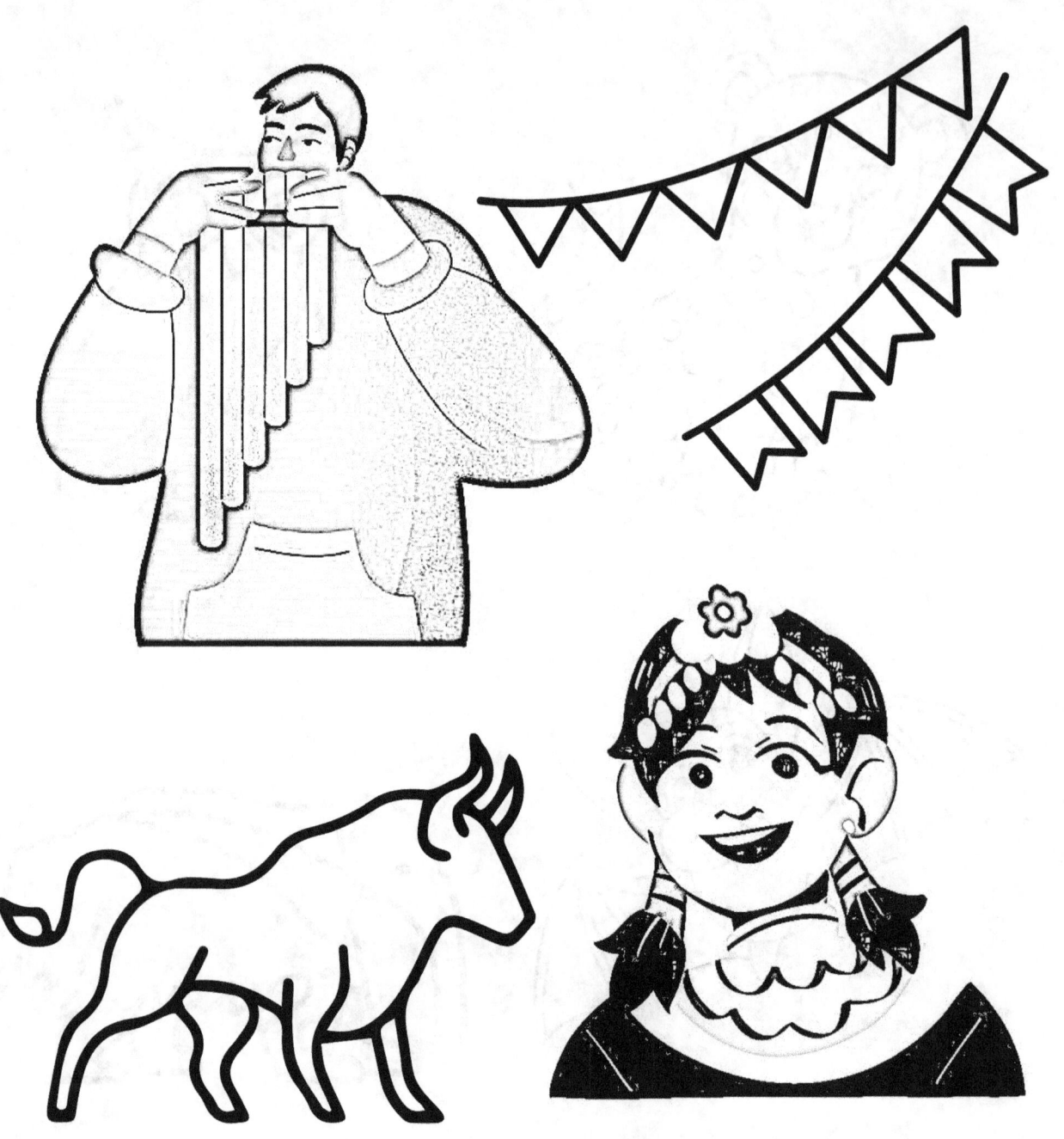

The local festivals have folkloric dances, bullfights, games, culture, and tourism fairs. The carnival in the city of Trinidad is celebrated with the joy typical of the Moxeño towns (a prehispanic culture).

Cochabamba

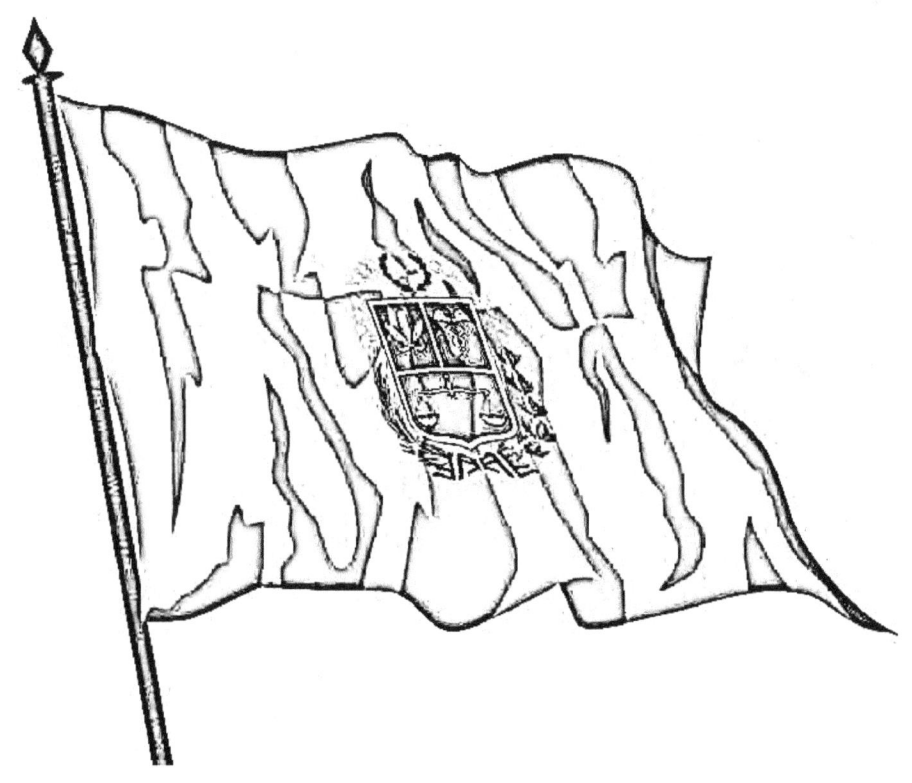

Cochabamba's flag color is sky blue, and it has a coat of arms in the middle of it.

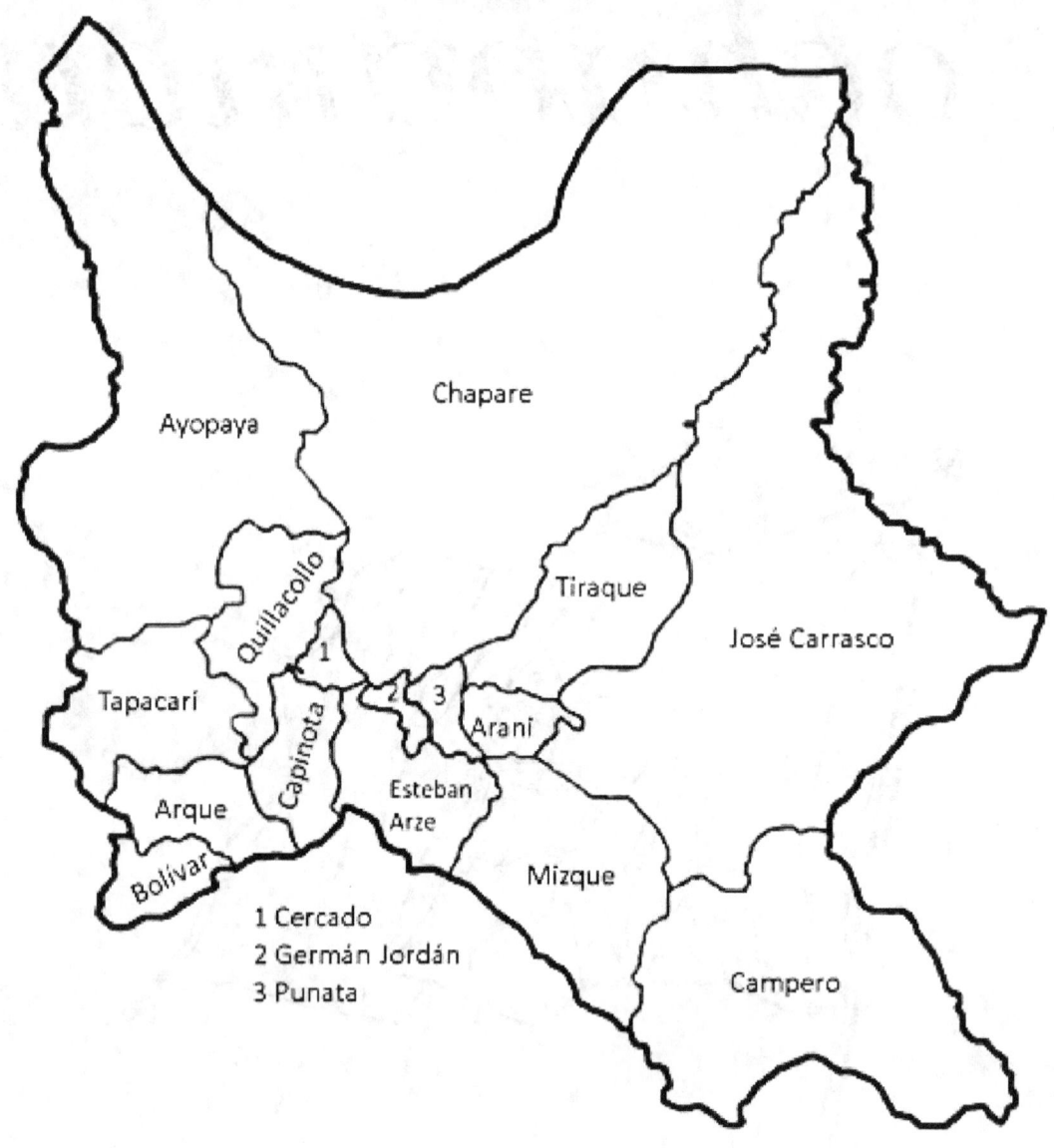

It is located in the center of the country and its territory covers part of the Elbow of the Andes, the inter-Andean valleys and the tropical plains. Cochabamba, also called; "Garden City of Bolivia" for its beautiful landscapes and parks

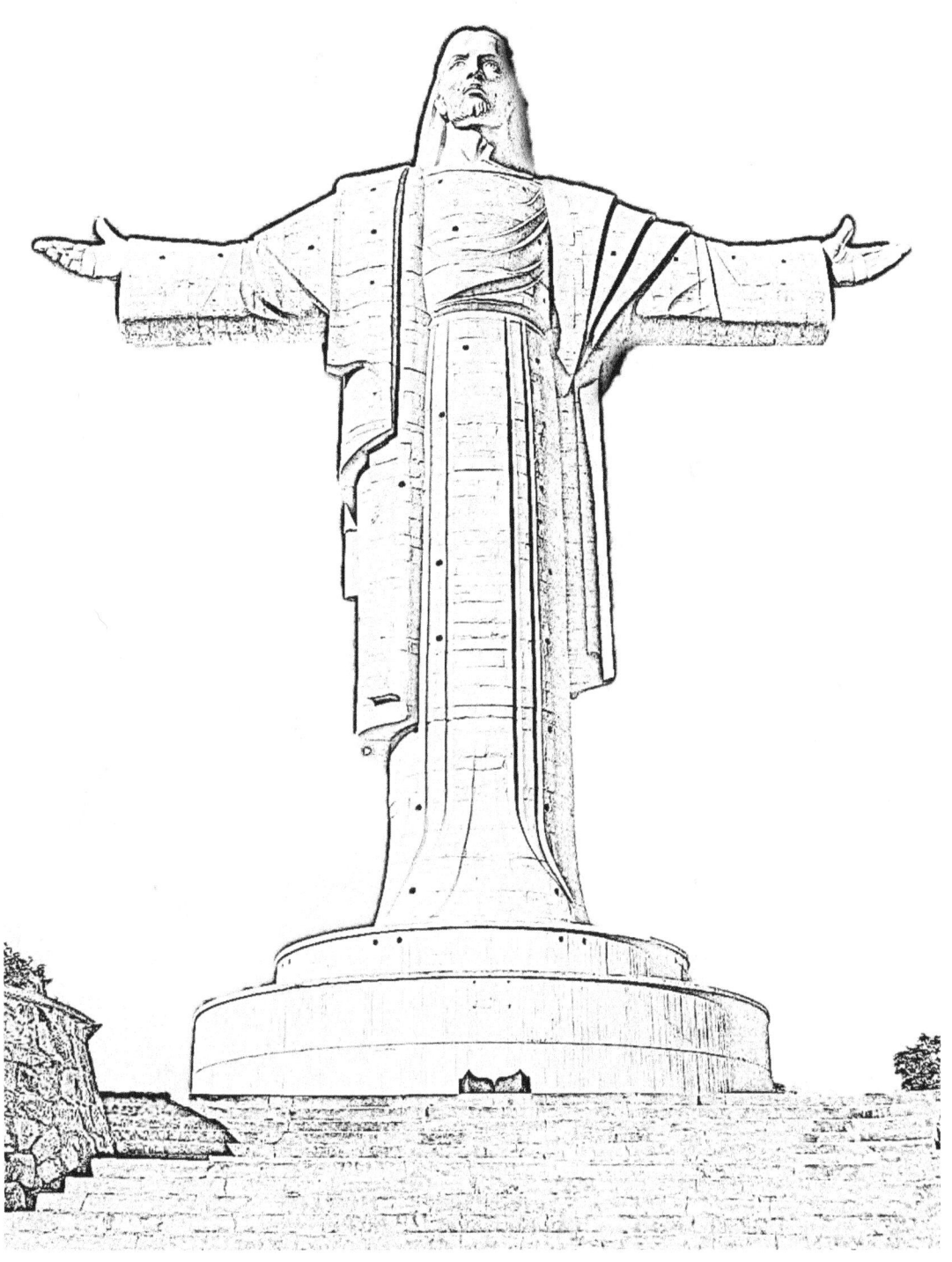

Cochabamba has Cristo de la Concordia which is a statue of Jesus Christ located on top of a hill. it is the third largest statue of Jesus Christ in the world.

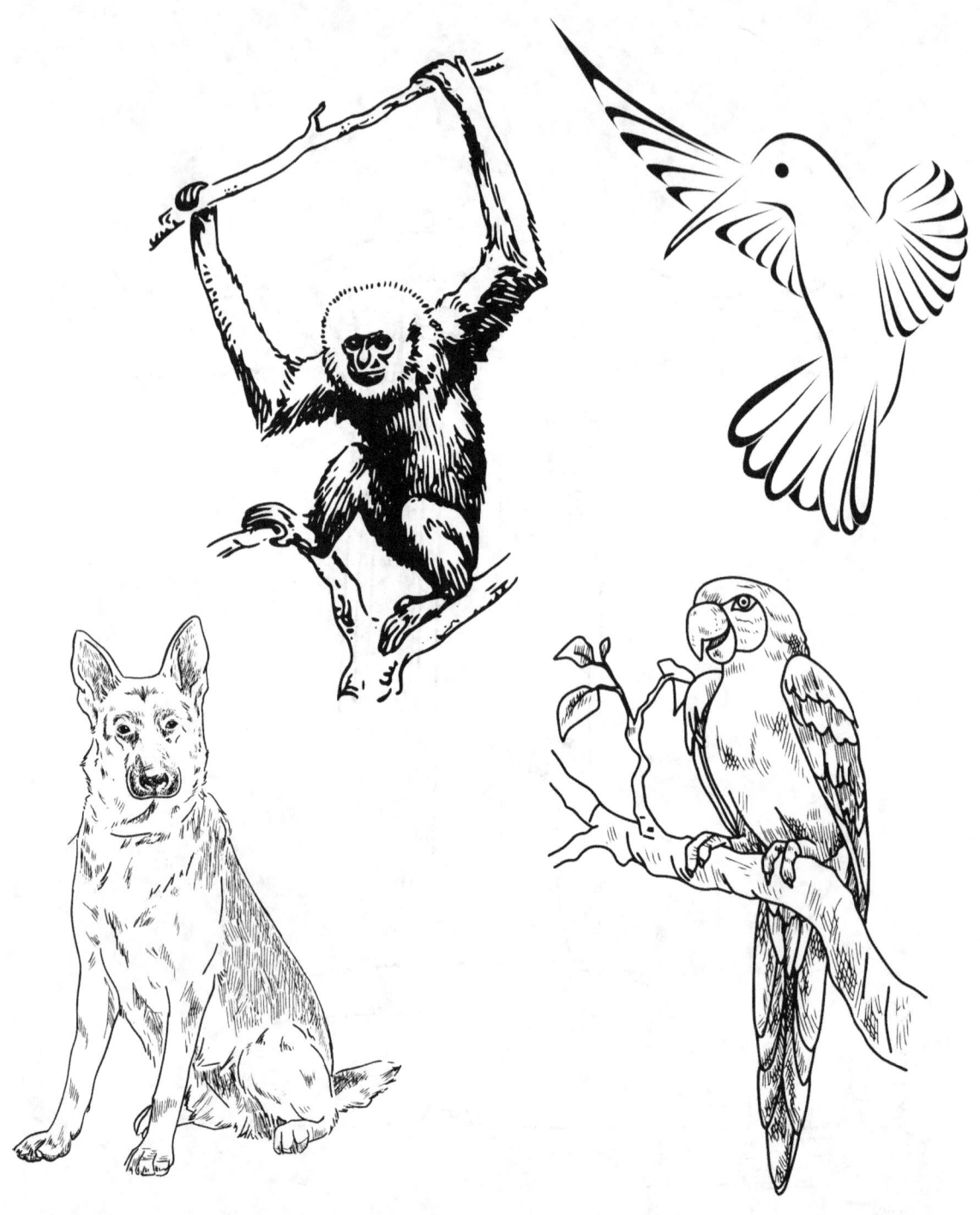

Cochabamba's fauna includes:
Jaguars, Pumas, Troop Pigs, Wild Dogs, Swamp Deer, Bufeos, Londras, Titi Monkeys, Wildcats, Parrots, Toucans, Hawks, Ducks, Herons, etc.

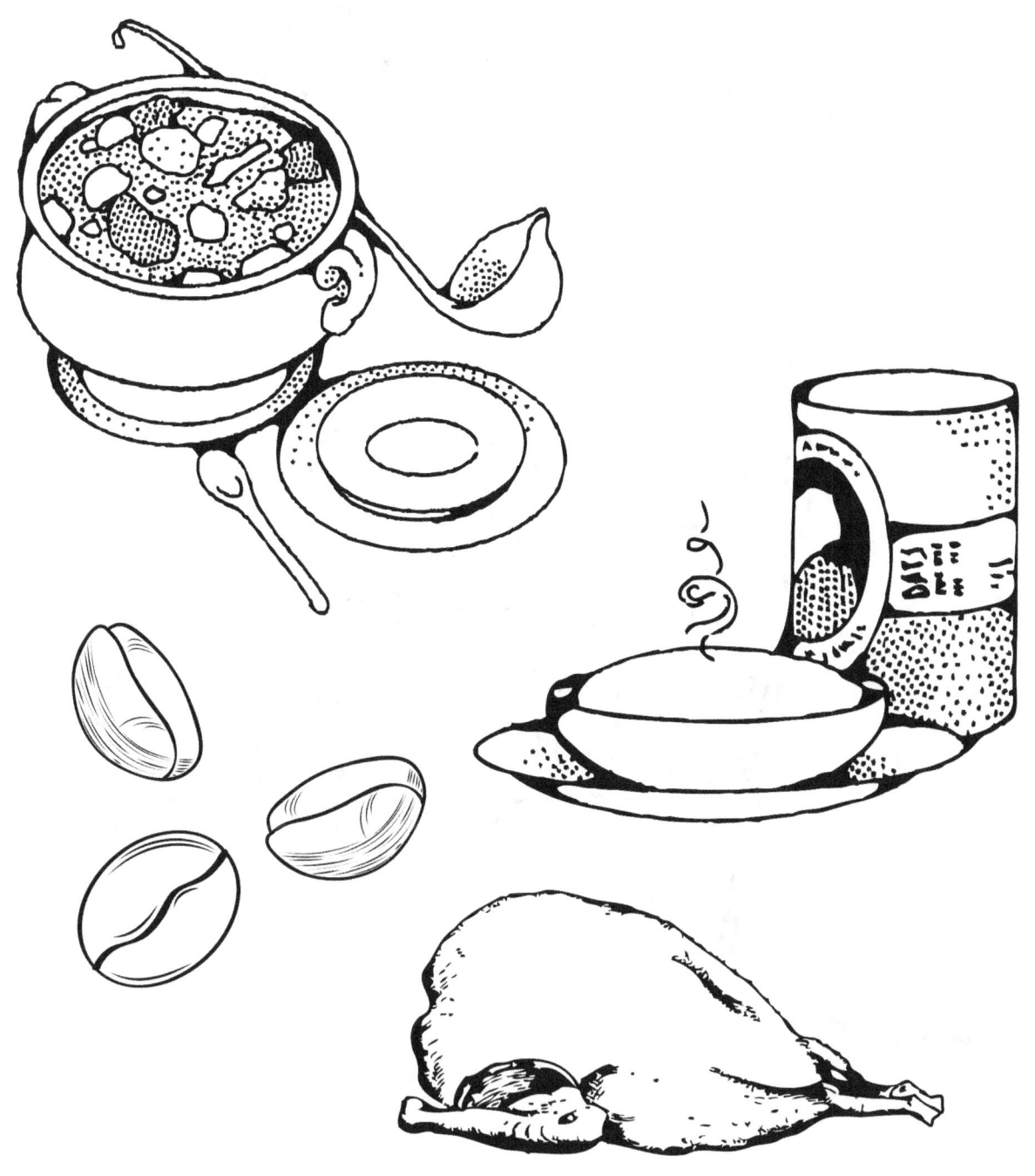

Typical dishes from the department Pampaku, Silpancho, Jaka Lawa (soup), Habas Pecktu, Pique a lo macho (meat, sausages, fries, udders, salad), Charque and the local coffee production is a growing industry.

Santa Cruz

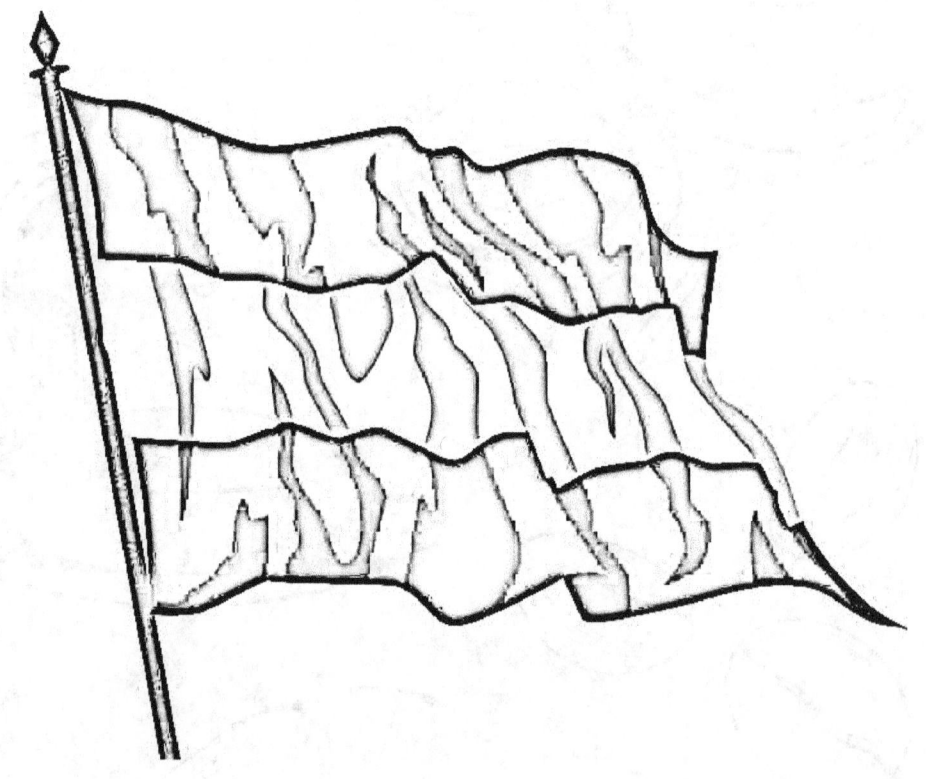

Santa Cruz's flag has three horizontal stripes. The top and bottom stripes are green and the middle stripe is white with the coat of arms.

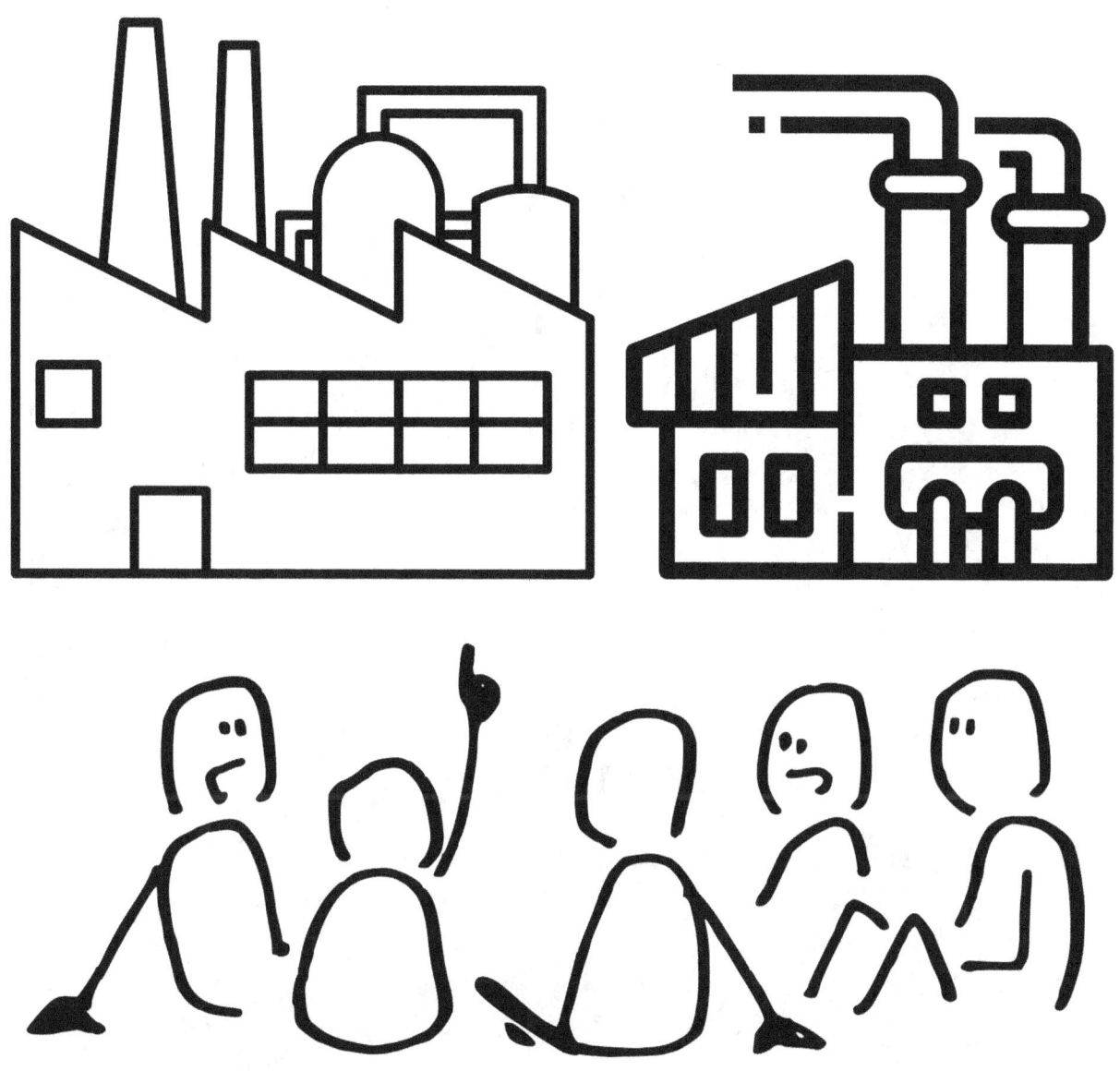

It is the most industrialized region of Bolivia. It is the largest and it is the most populous department in Bolivia

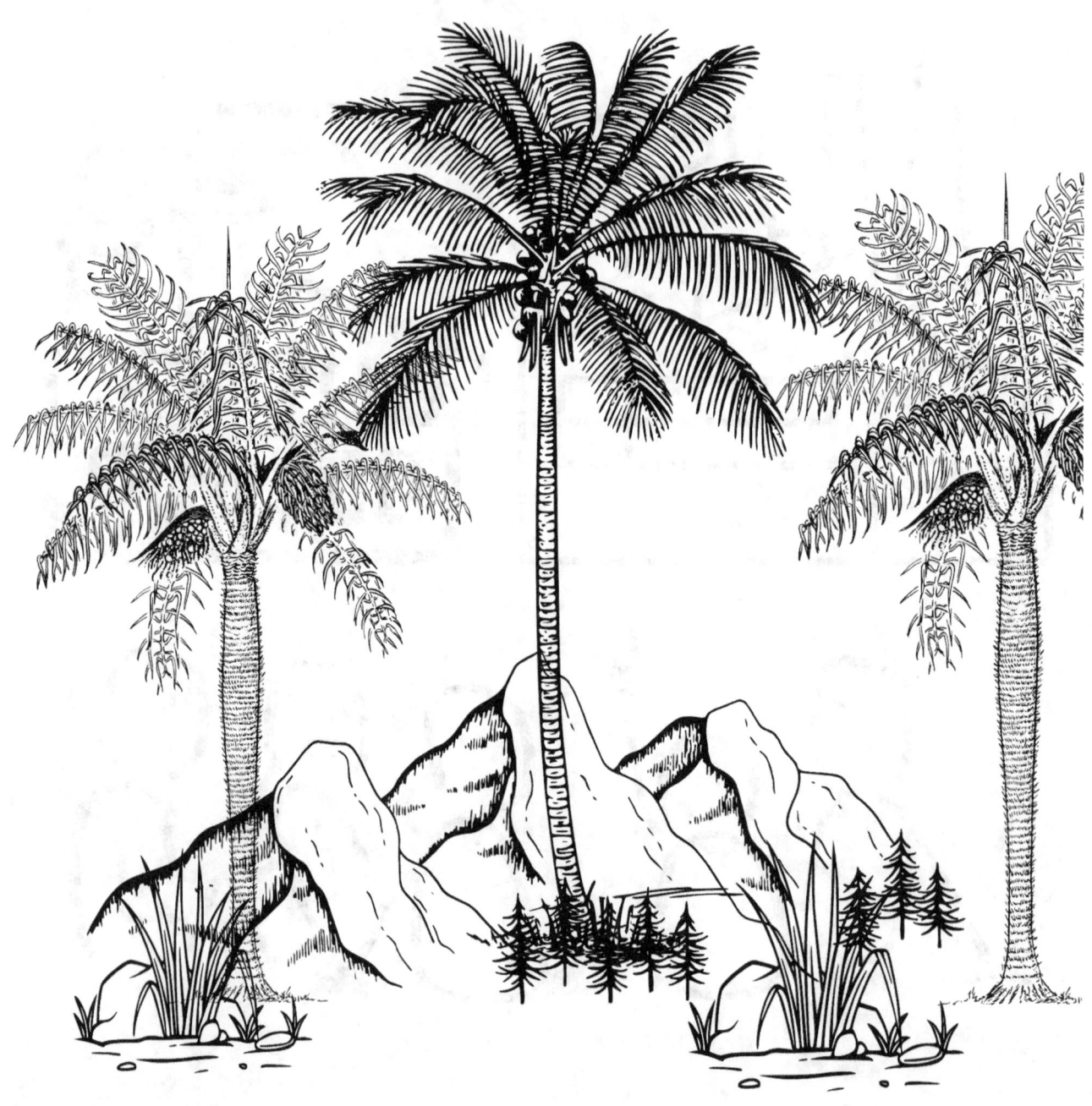

Santa Cruz is a tropical paradise in Bolivia, a department of exuberant vegetation with vast expanses of jungle and grasslands (part of the amazon), located in the eastern part of the Bolivian territory.

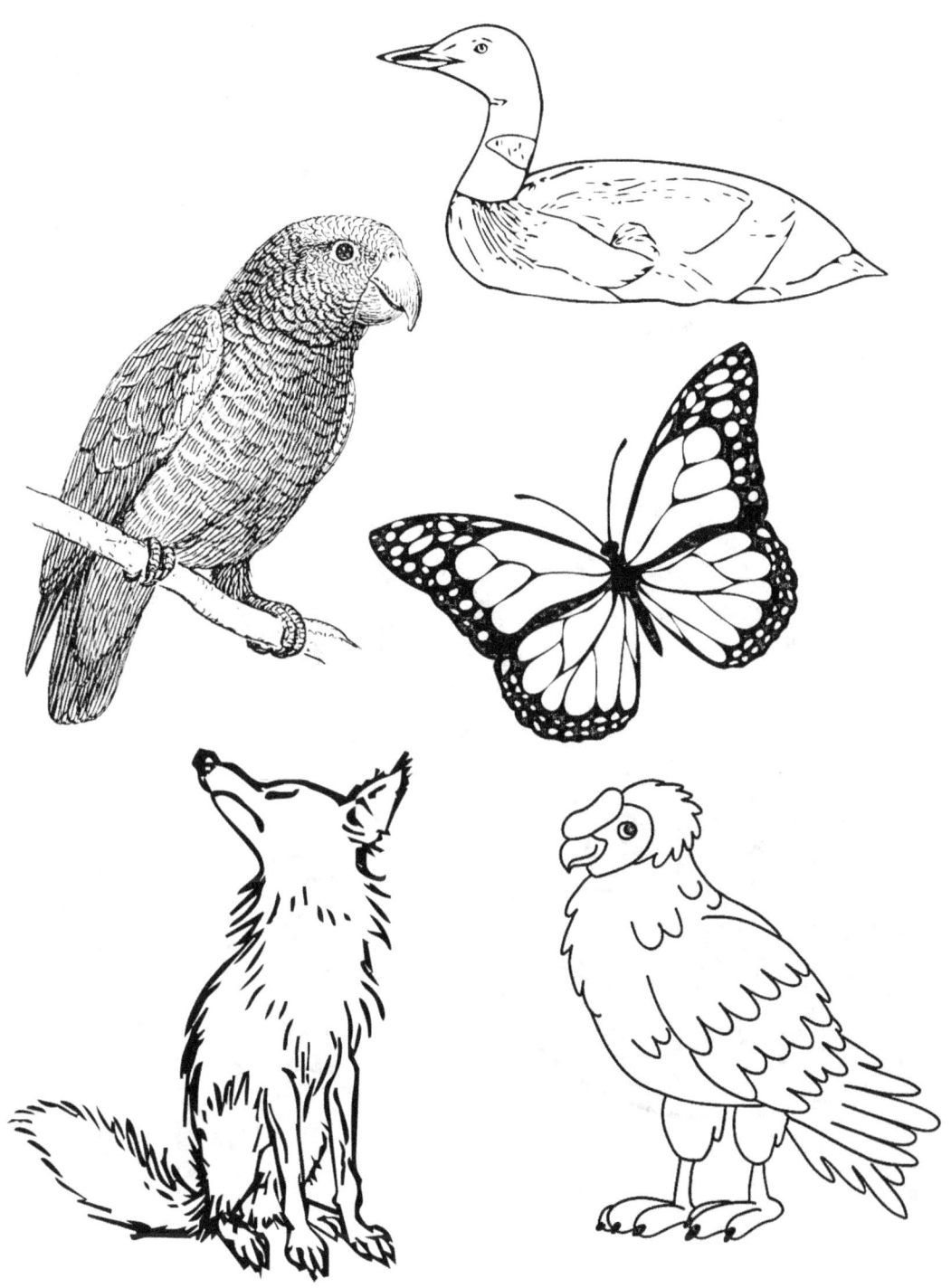

The fauna is represented by the puma, red and gray fox, butterflies, guanaco, ñandú. Its abundant birdlife is made up of the condor, the Moorish eagle, black-necked swan, hummingbird.

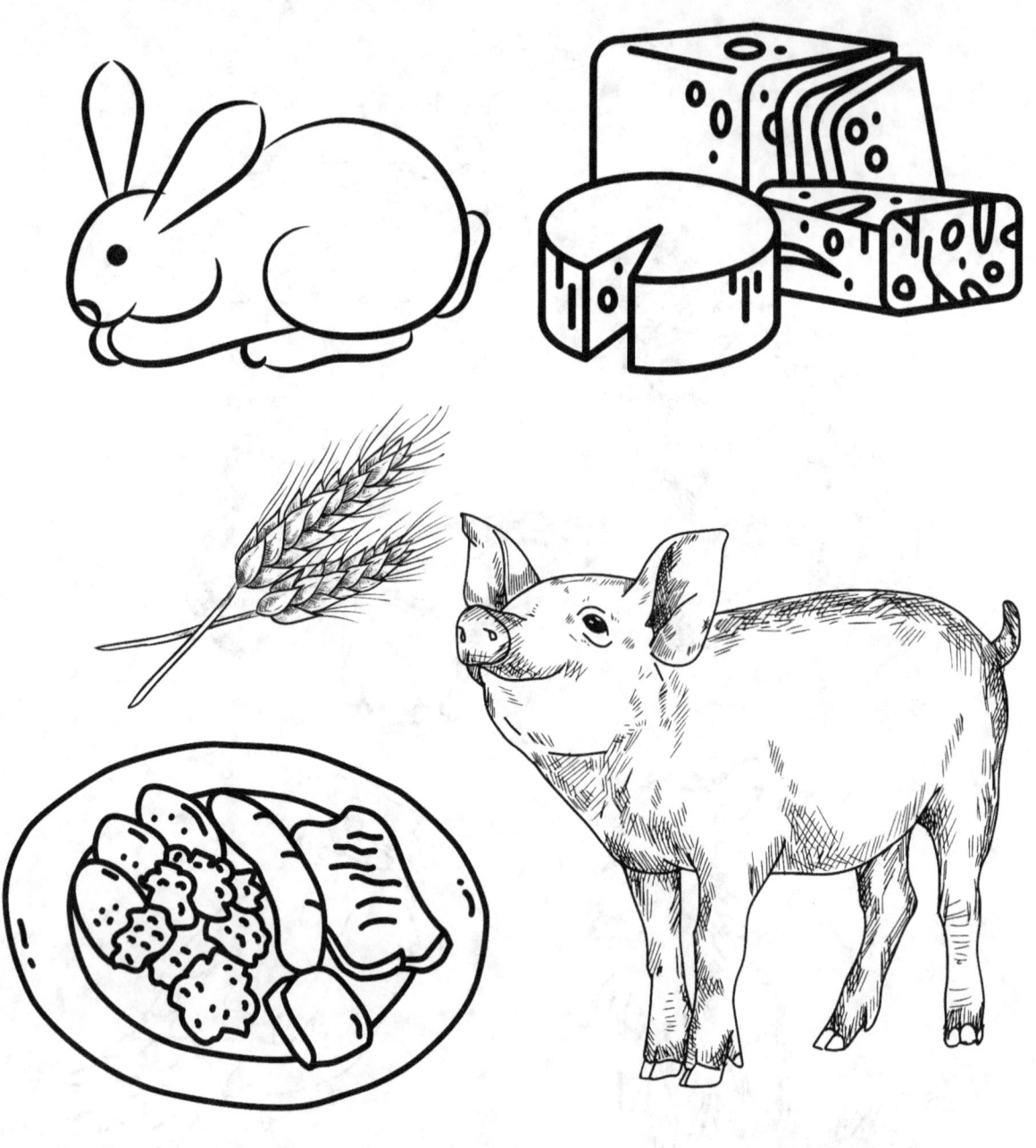

Typical dishes from the department: Majao, Locro, Zonzo, Cuñape, Jochi Pintao, Keperí, Pacumuto, Asadito colorado, Patasca, Masaco de platano.

Potosí

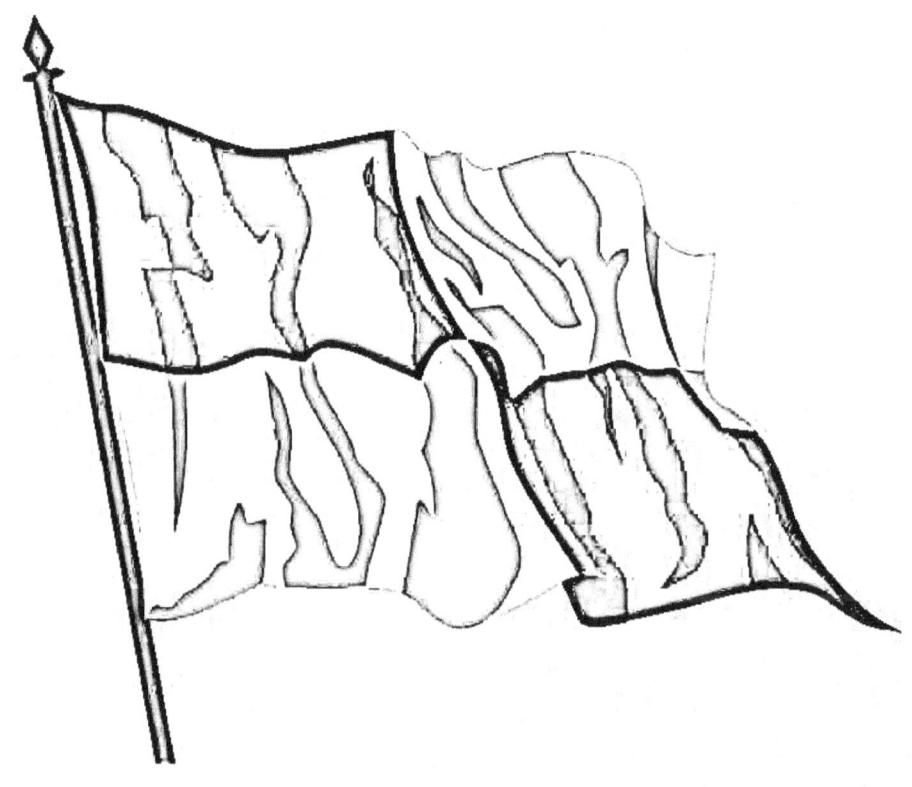

Potosi's flag has 1 red square and 1 white square at the top (left to right) and 1 white square and 1 red square at the bottom (left to right).

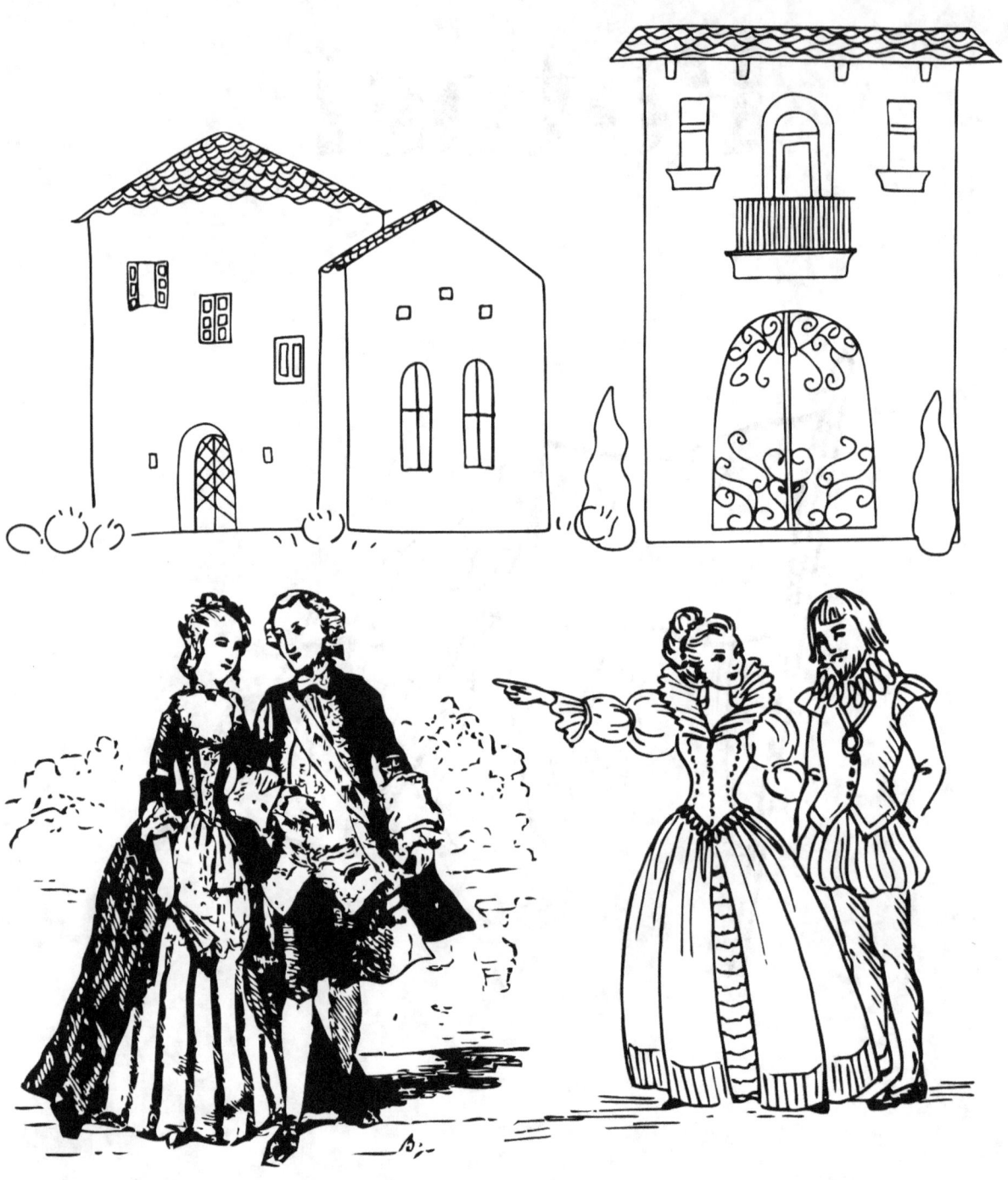

Potosí was the most populated city in the world with about 160,000 inhabitants. In the year 1650 it had a population greater than cities like London, Paris or Madrid.

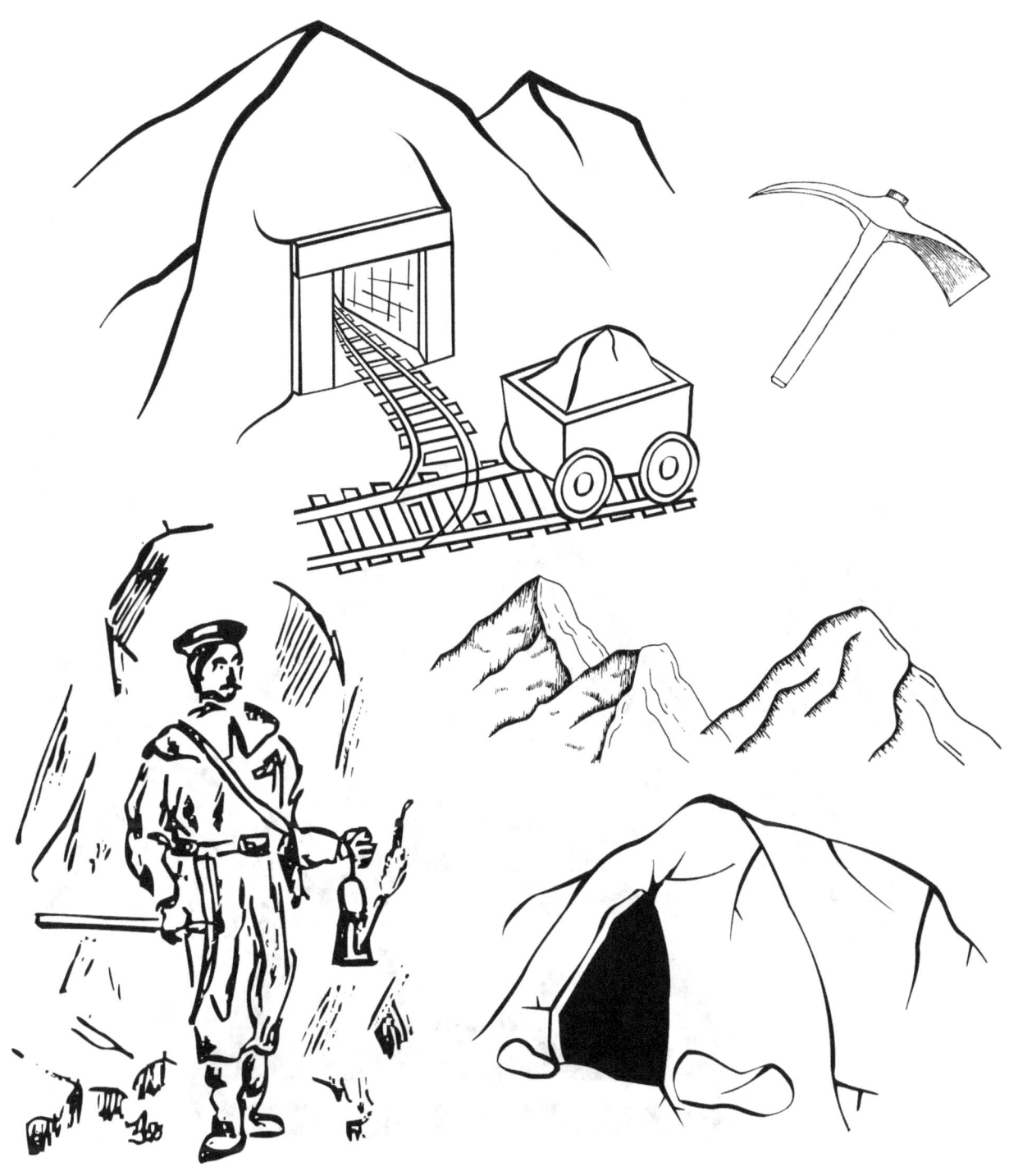

Mining constitutes the main economic activity of the department. the silver deposits made it famous, the subsoil still holds numerous mineral wealth.

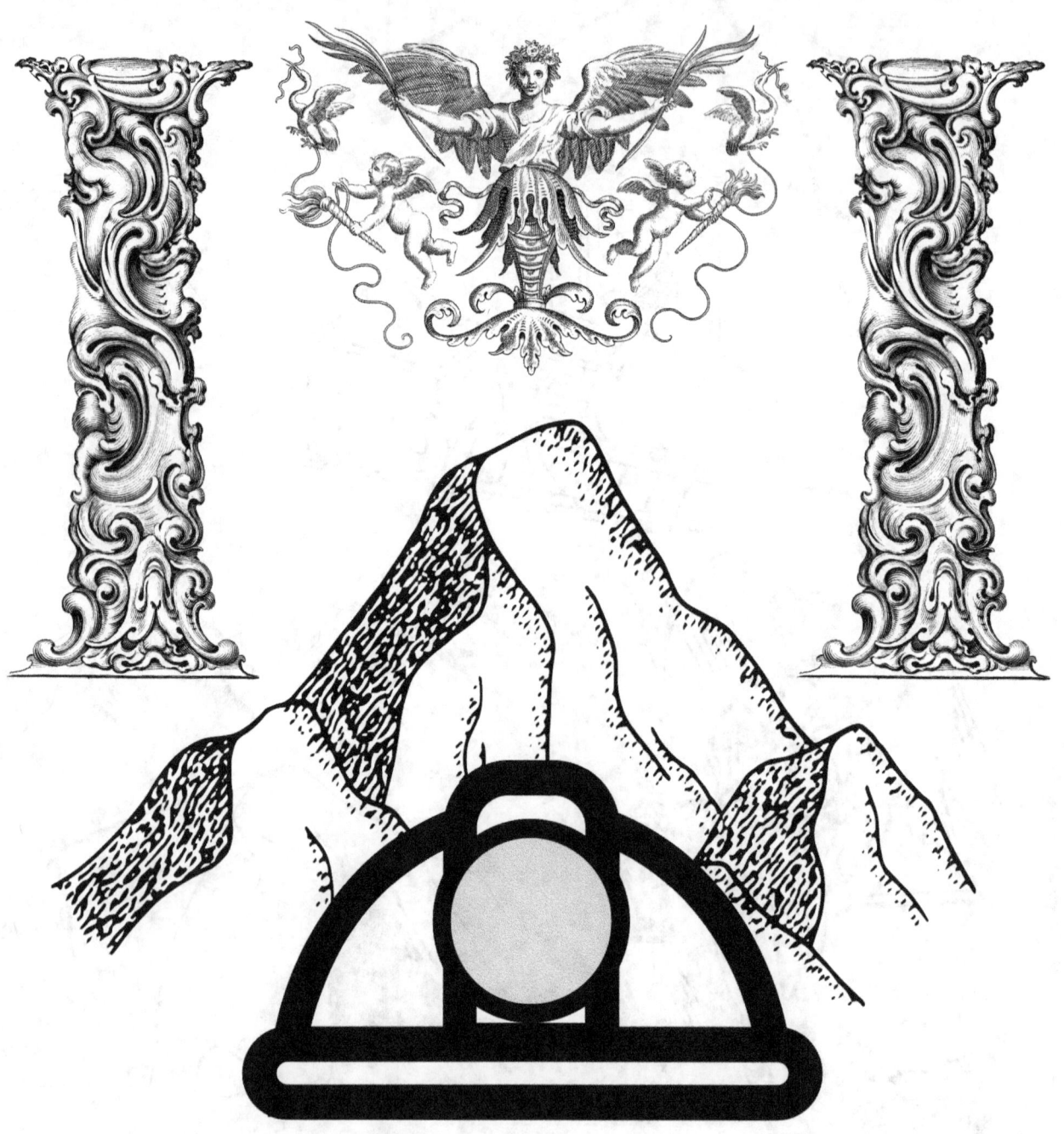

It was declared a World Heritage Site in 1987 due to its contribution to universal history and its architectural and artistic appeal, being considered the cradle of the Andean baroque in Bolivia.

SALTEÑA

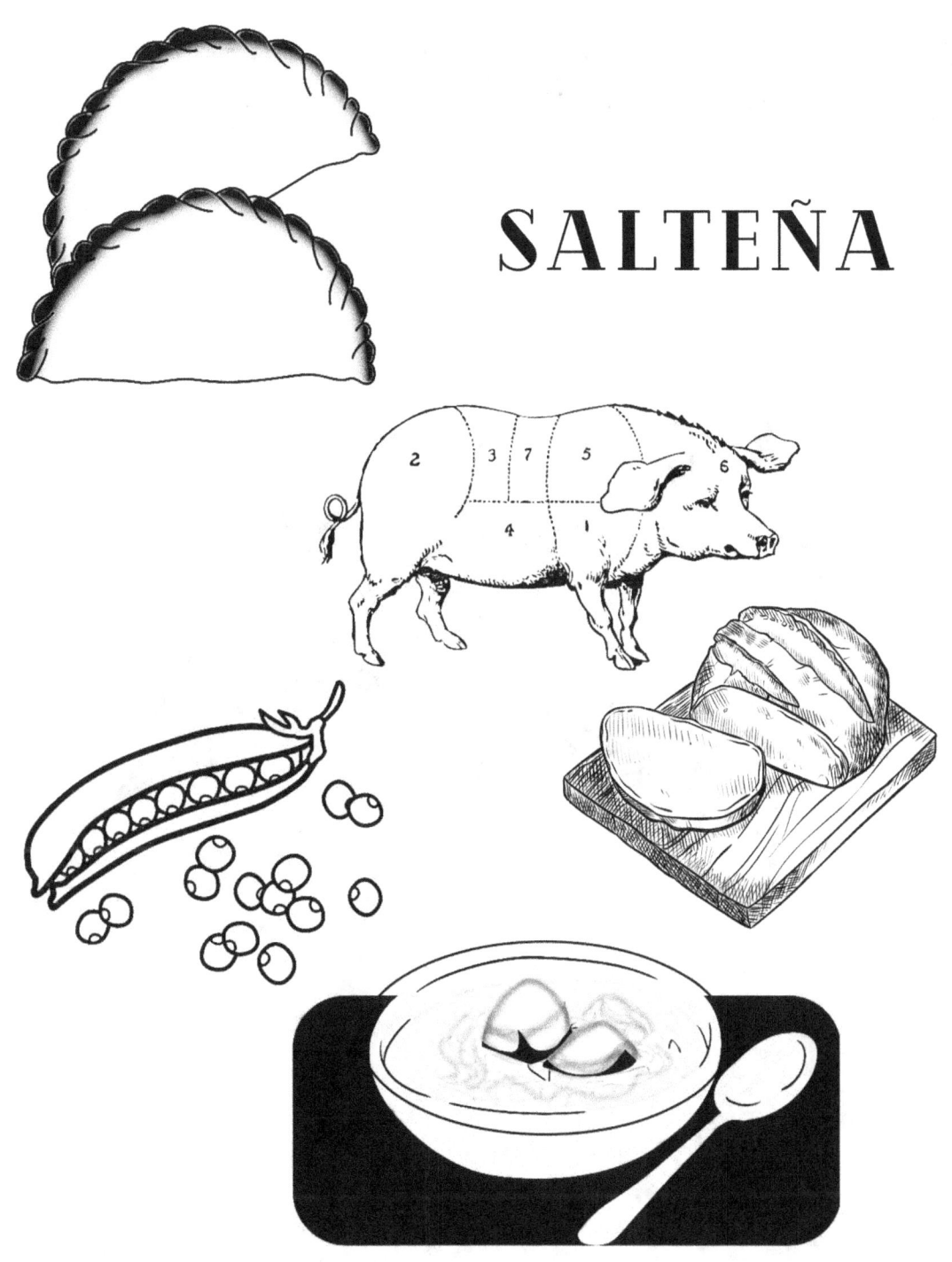

Typical dishes from this department: Calapurka, Chambergos, Chajchu, Sopaipillas, Salteña, Ají de arvejas, Confites, Chapu minero, Ají de Pataskha.

Chuquisaca

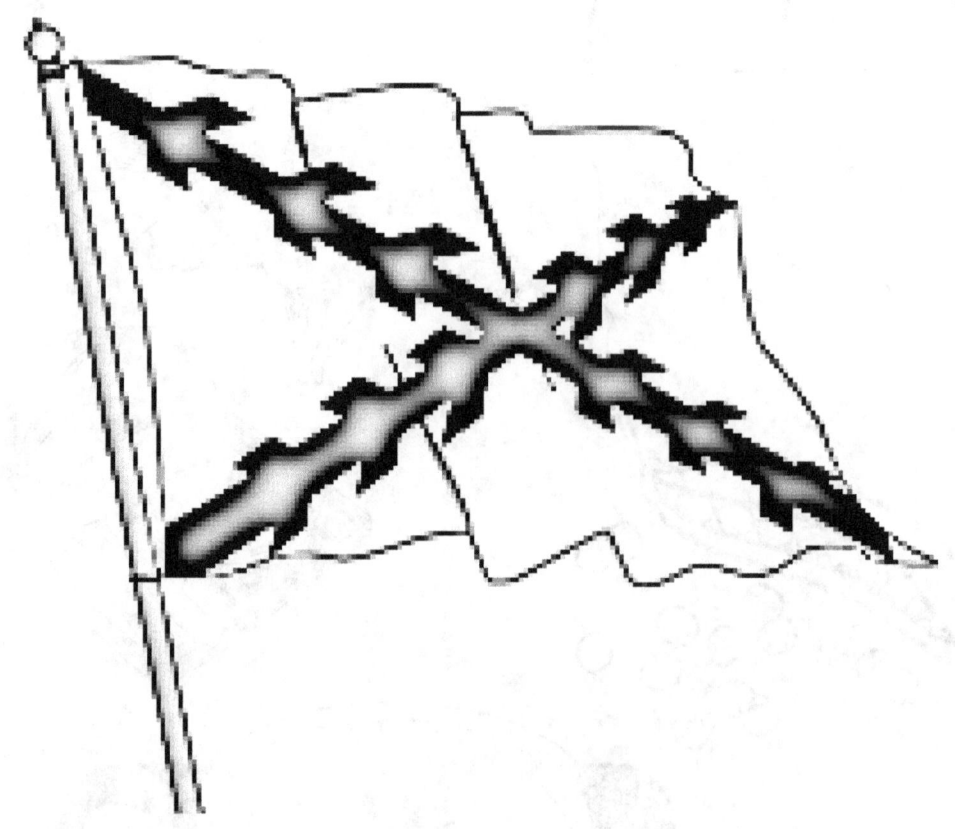

Chuquisaca's flag is completely white, crisscrossed from end to end by two arrow-shaped red stripes, thus joining the four corners.

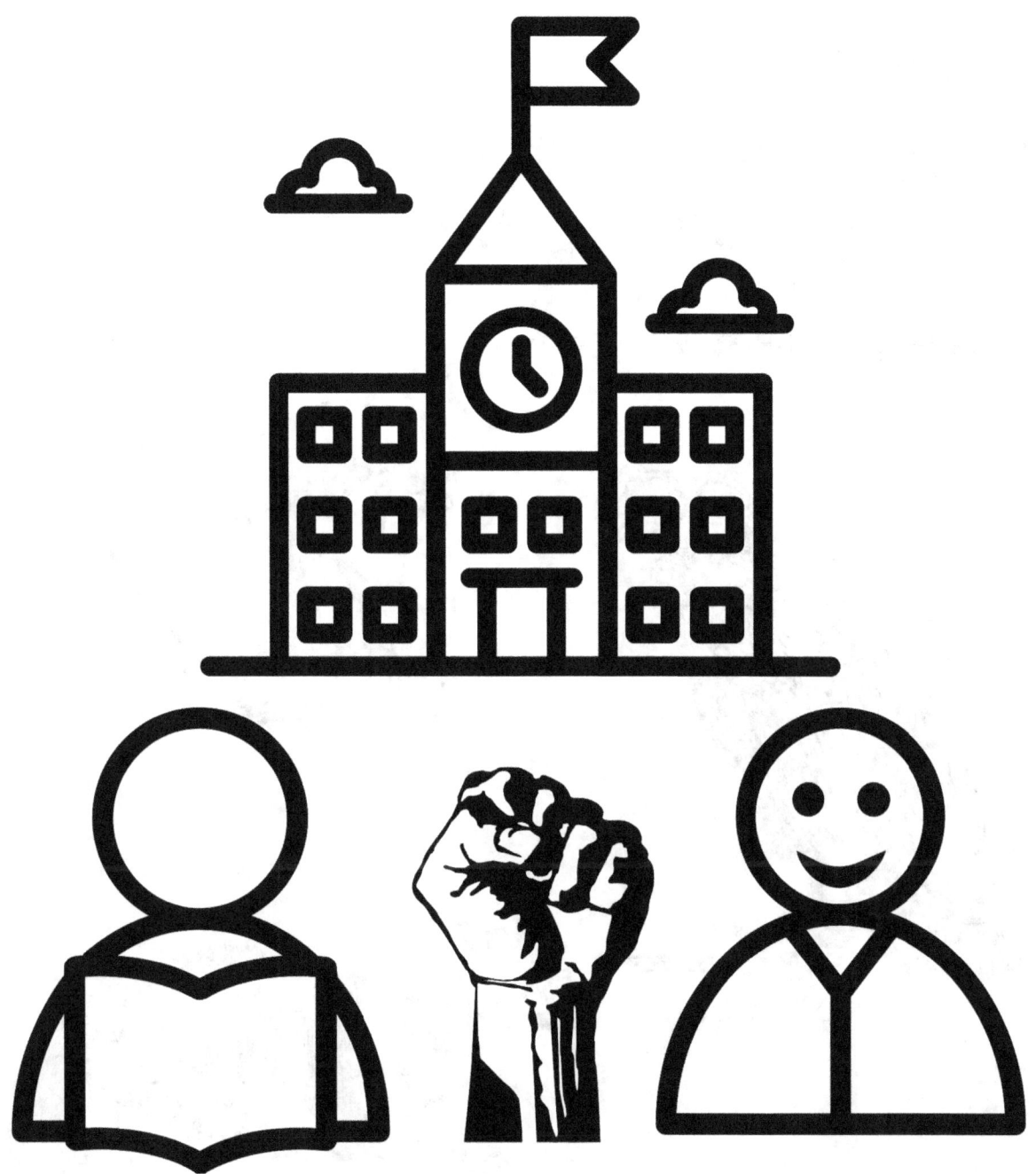

Bolivia's oldest university is Universidad de San Francisco Xavier de Chuquisaca and it was at the heart of the nation's battle for independence and remains an animated hive for the nation's students.

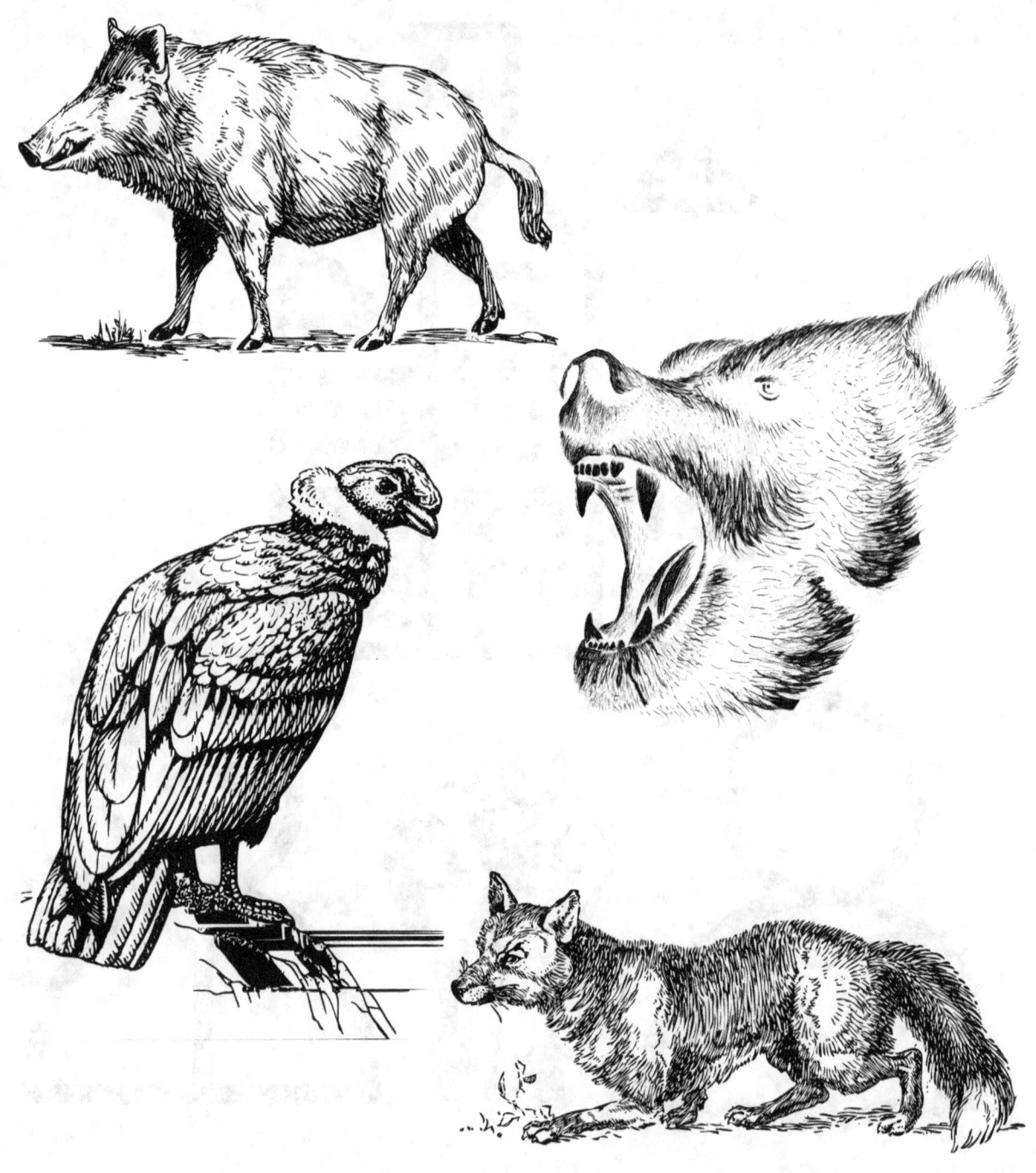

Chuquisaca's fauna: The (Jucumari) bear, the puma, the pajonal or titi cat, the wild pig (Pecarí del Chaco), the fox, etc. Birds: the Condor, Eagles, Hawks, Vultures, Woodpeckers, etc.

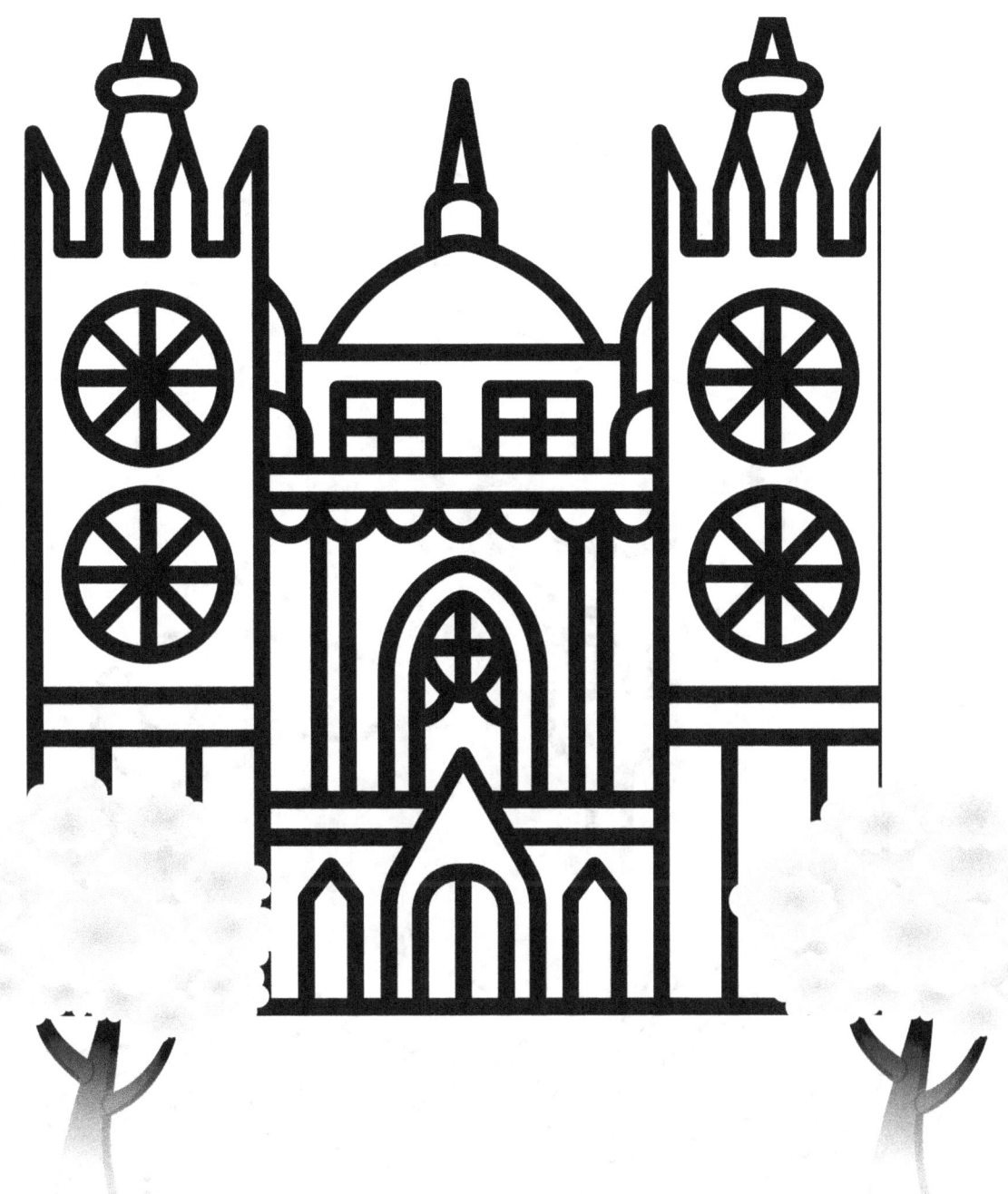

The Cathedral Basilica of Our Lady of Guadalupe occupies one of the corners of Plaza (sqare) 25 de Mayo.
It has various architectural styles since its construction period was long, between 1551 and the early 1700s.

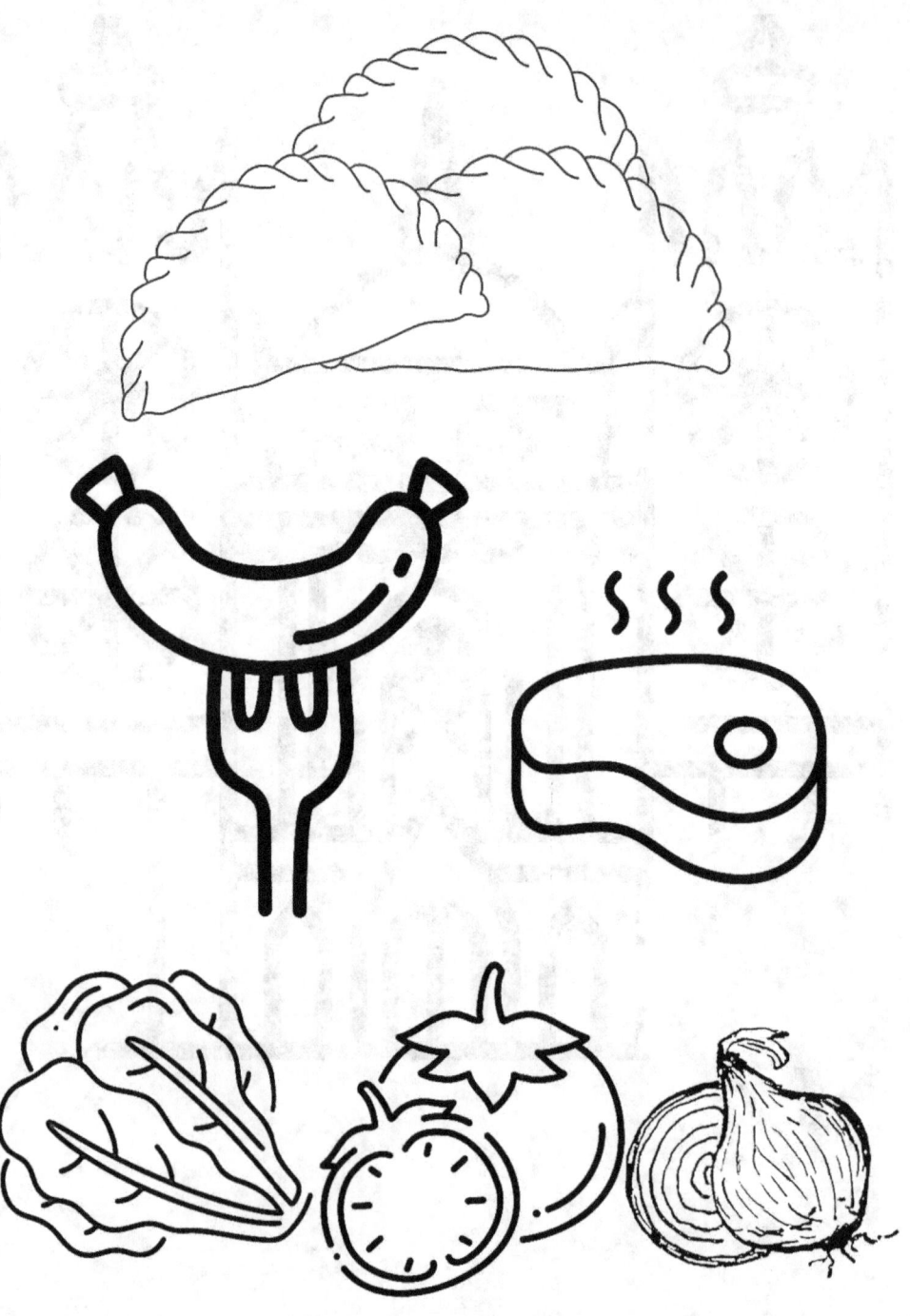

Typical dishes: Chorizos Chuquisaqueños (sausages) ,Fritanga, Mondongo ,K'arapecho, Coco de Pollo, Sulka, salteña chuquisaqueña (empanada shape with salteñas filling).

Tarija

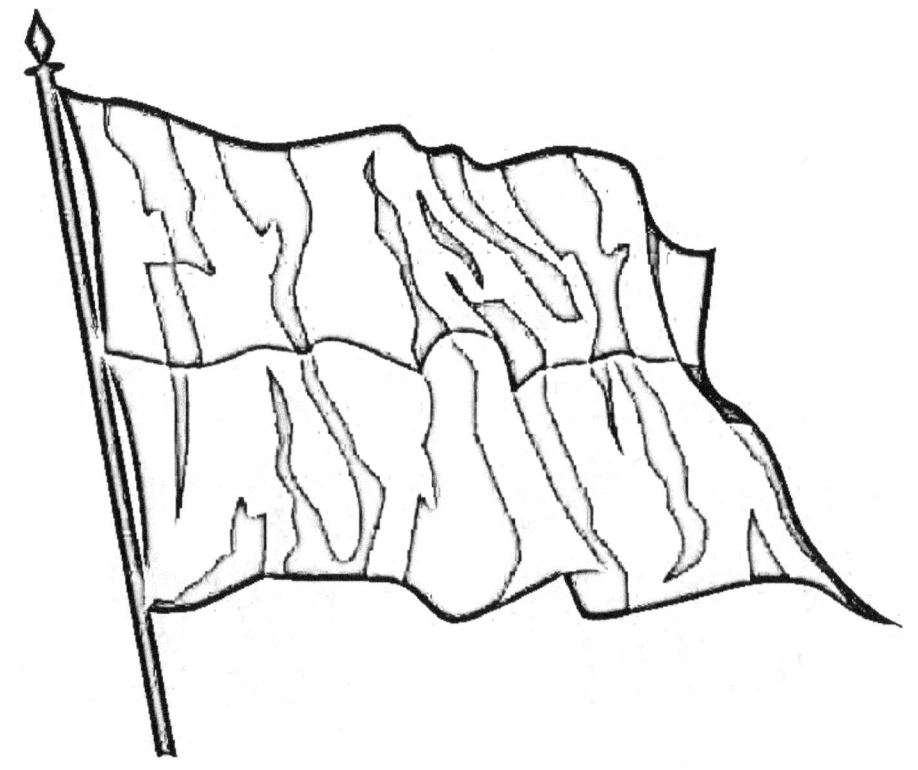

Tarija's flag has two symmetrical horizontal stripes(of equal dimensions), the upper one is red in color and the lower stripe is white with the coat of arms.

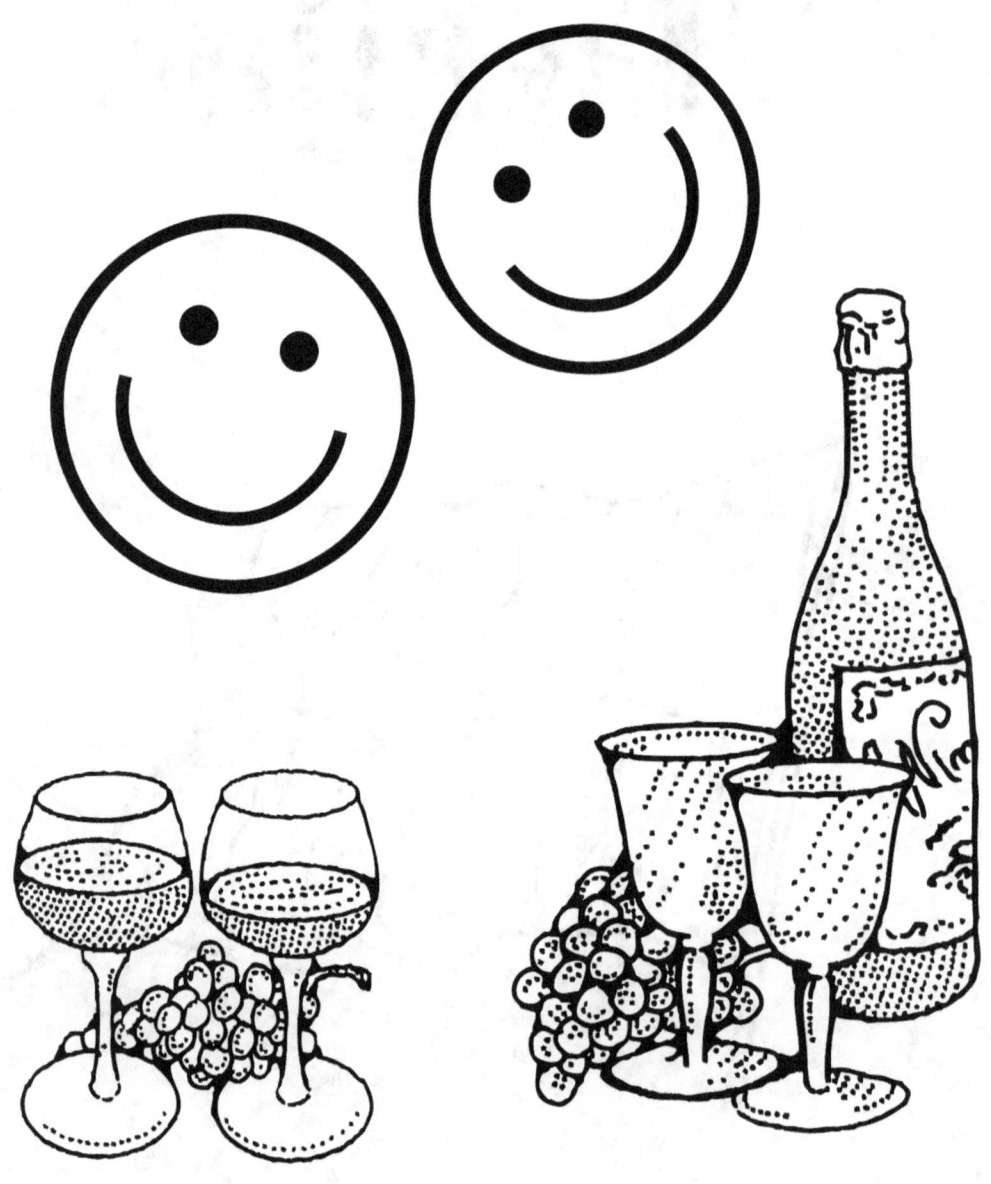

The city of Tarija, known as "the capital of the smile", it is characterized by the hospitality of its people, for having very pleasant climate, and for its wine production. The wine industry and the hydrocarbons industry constitute the two economic pillars of the department.

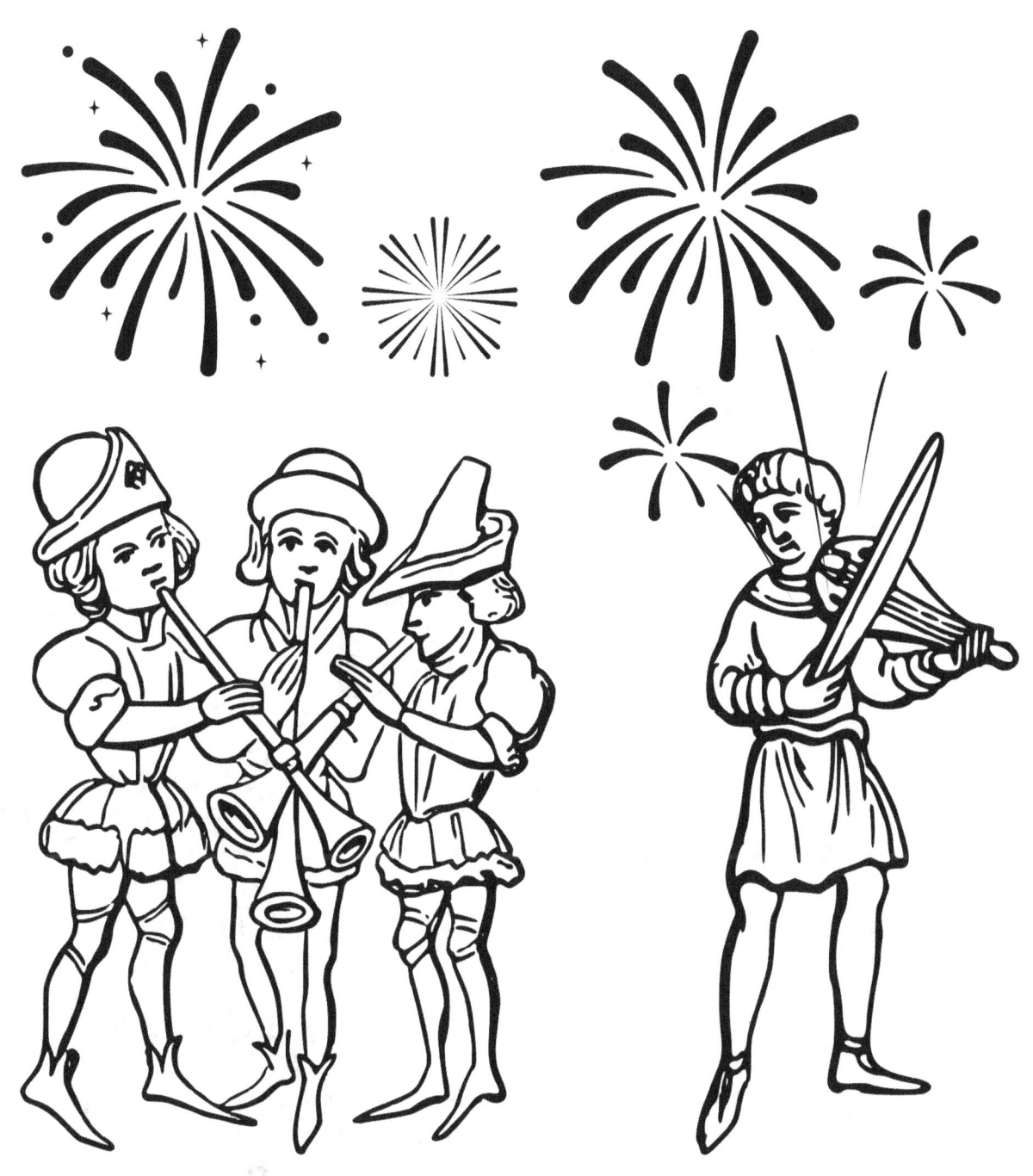

The Fiesta Grande de Tarija (Big Party of Tarija) takes place in the city of the same name, it is celebrated every year in the months of August and September with a whole series of religious processions, music festivals, dances, competitions and fireworks in honor of (Saint) San Roque.

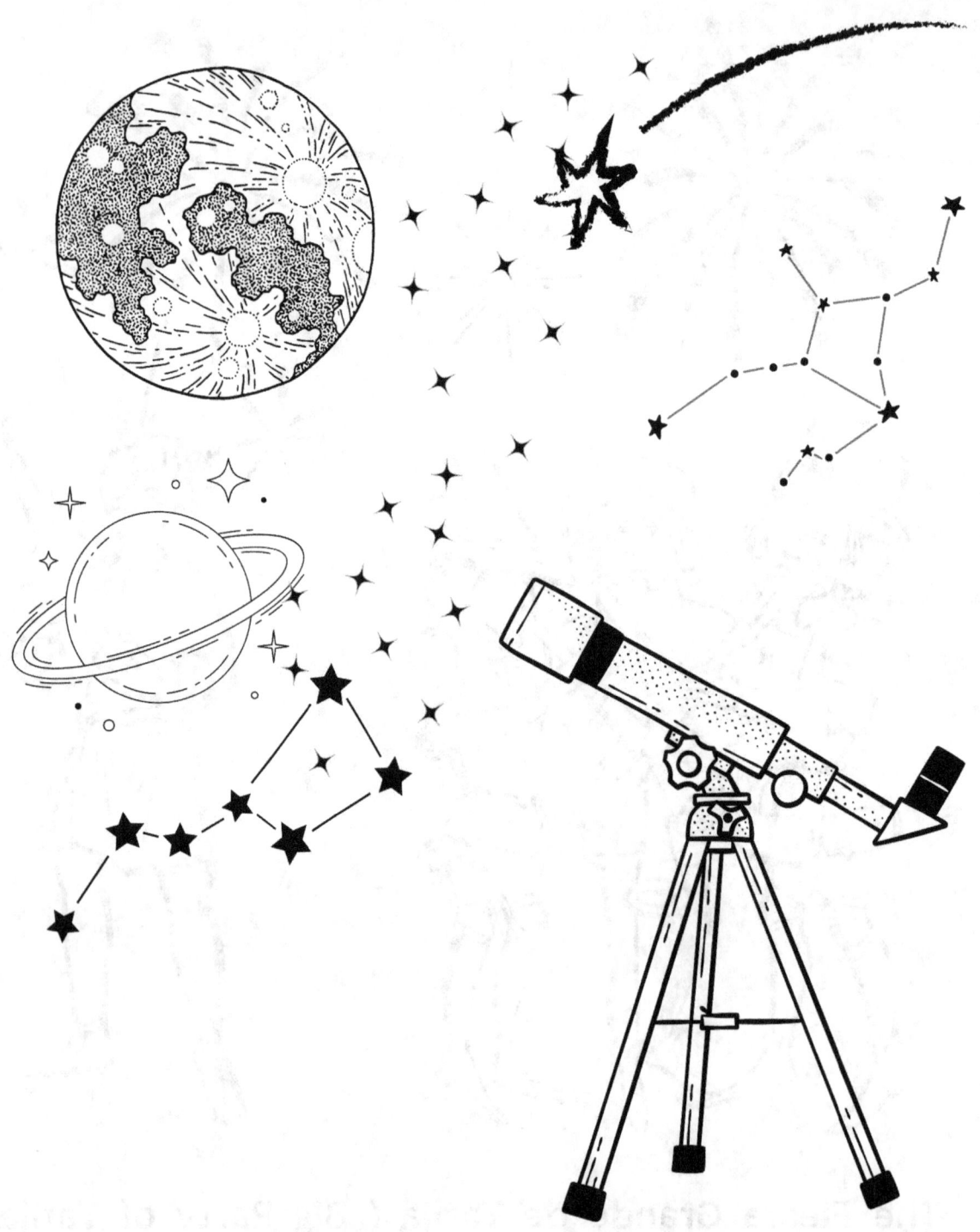

Located in the town of Santa Ana is the country's Astronomical Observatory, which has two telescopes of Russian origin and an atomic clock that marks the official Bolivian time.

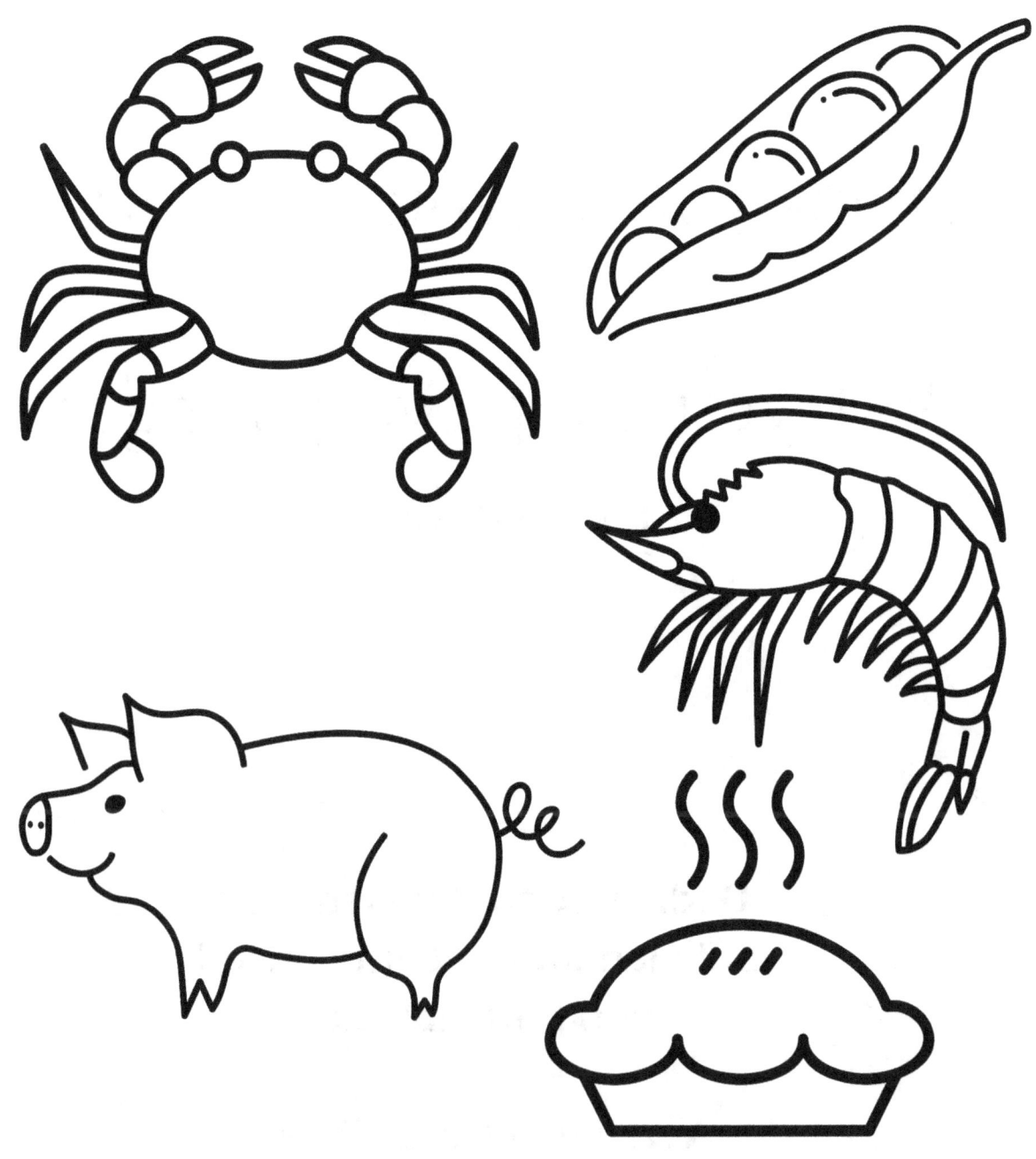

Typical dishes from Tarija are : Ranga Ranga, Arvejada, Huminta a la Piedra, Chupe de camaroncillo de río, Pig on Cross, BBQ beef.

Thank you for your support !

With your help everything is possible.

Dedicated to Bolivians and Bolivian descendants raised and born abroad.

Viva mi patria Bolivia !

Book imagined and put together by : SAE